The Path to Holiness

Copyright © 2024 by JZ Maille
All rights reserved. Printed in the United States of America.
No part of this book may be reproduced in any form or by any electronic or mechanical means, including information storage and retrieval systems, without written permission from the author, except for the use of brief quotations in a book review.
Scriptures quotations are taken from the Bibles: Douay-Rheims 1899 American edition (DRA) and New Revised Standard Version Catholic Edition (NRSVCE)
Images: KajzrPhotography/shutterstock.com
Fotokita/shutterstock.com
conrado/shutterstock.com

This publication has been translated in Spanish under the title: El Camino a la Santidad: guía para catolicos en un mundo pagano.
for information contact:
thepathtoholiness.com
jzmaille@gmail.com

Library of Congress Control Number: 2024911266

ISBN Paperback 979-8-9906227-0-8
ebook: 979-8-9906227-2-2
Hard Cover: 979-8-9906227-1-5

My lovely husband, you are my soulmate, the love of my life, and the worst at choosing movies. Your unwavering support has made this book possible, and I am forever grateful for your love and encouragement.

To my readers:
May your pursuit of holiness be as relentless as your attachment to mortal life. Kindly keep me in your prayers if you find this book helpful, and pray even harder if you don't.

"for without me you can do nothing."

— JOHN 15:5

CONTENTS

INTRODUCTION ... ix

1. THE SAINTS OF THE CATHOLIC CHURCH ... 1
2. ATTAINING HOLINESS ... 5
3. THE GRACE OF GOD ... 12
4. THE ENEMIES OF HOLINESS ... 15
5. UNDERSTANDING GOD'S WILL ... 17
   14 STEPS TO HOLINESS ... 23
6. STEP ONE ... 24
   THE SURRENDER OF THE FREE WILL
   AGREEMENT ... 31
7. STEP TWO ... 32
   SACRAMENTAL CONFESSION
   AGREEMENT ... 37
8. STEP THREE ... 38
   REPARATIONS FOR OUR SINS
   AGREEMENT ... 43
9. STEP FOUR ... 44
   DETACHMENT FROM WORLDLY THINGS
   AGREEMENT ... 53
10. STEP FIVE ... 54
    HOLY MASS AND EUCHARISTIC COMMUNION
    AGREEMENT ... 71
11. STEP SIX ... 72
    EUCHARISTIC ADORATION OF THE BLESSED SACRAMENT
    AGREEMENT ... 77
12. STEP SEVEN ... 78
    THE HOLY ROSARY
    AGREEMENT ... 89
13. STEP EIGHT ... 90
    INTERCESSORY PRAYER
    AGREEMENT ... 93
14. STEP NINE ... 94
    THE COMMANDMENTS

AGREEMENT	97
15. STEP TEN	98
BIBLE READING	
AGREEMENT	107
16. STEP ELEVEN	108
PIOUS PRACTICES AND DEVOTIONS	
AGREEMENT	133
17. STEP TWELVE	134
Praying All Day Long	
AGREEMENT	137
18. STEP THIRTEEN	138
FASTING	
AGREEMENT	141
19. STEP FOURTEEN	142
HOME ALTAR AND THE USE OF SACRAMENTALS	
AGREEMENT	147
20. THE FRUITS OF HOLINESS	148
21. HOLINESS IN OTHER RELIGIONS	161
22. SALVATION IN OTHER RELIGIONS	175
23. KEEPING UP WITH OUR JOURNEY TO HOLINESS	188
24. REFLECTION	191
Take me Home	193
About the Author	195
Also by JZ Maille	197
Notes	199

INTRODUCTION

* * *

Here I am, a sinner attempting to write a book about holiness. I must confess that I am far from being a saint myself, and my pursuit of holiness is still a work in progress. However, I believe that I don't have to be holy to help others. After all, who can truly claim to be holy? Not even the Saints knew they were holy until after their death. I am simply a concerned soul searching for the ultimate goal- Heaven.

Throughout my life, I have been on a quest to discover the true meaning of life. Like countless others, I have often wondered about the purpose of our existence and why we are here. As someone who grew up in the Catholic faith, I had the privilege and honor of meeting two remarkable saints: Saint Mother Teresa of Calcutta and Saint John Paul II.

I vividly recall the day that I met Mother Teresa. I was just a child, and I remember being pushed forward so she could touch me. At the time, I didn't fully understand the moment's significance. I just wanted to go back to my friends and play. However,

INTRODUCTION

looking back on that day, I now realize how blessed I was to have met such a remarkable individual. As for Saint John Paul II, I remember his incredibly soft hands. It was like being touched with a feather. His presence was overwhelming. I knew he was important, but something about him touched the deepest parts of my soul. Some people say I am a third-class relic because both have touched me. I find that amusing.

Since my childhood, I have always been an enthusiastic reader. From a very young age, I have been fascinated by books on various topics such as law, medicine, cooking, and history. However, the stories that have always captured my heart the most were the lives of the Saints. They were different from the other characters in the books I read, and I admired how they lived their lives and how Jesus would talk to them. I yearned for a profound connection with Jesus and believed that if I became a Saint, he would speak to me, too.

At the age of 12, I embarked on a challenge to read the entire Bible, word by word, page by page. It was a daunting task, but I was determined to complete it. By age 13, my admiration for the saints had grown so much that I wanted to become a nun. I felt it was the best way to attain the connection with Jesus I so desperately craved. However, my desire faded away as I entered adolescence, and I was lost in a world of complete darkness. I drifted away from the church and stayed away for 20 years. Despite being unfaithful, God granted me the grace to return to His church. I believe that my encounter with two remarkable Saints was one of the tools God used to rescue me from paganism and the New Age. I credit this grace to the daily rosaries that I used to pray during my childhood and the intercessory prayers done on my behalf by the Church of Christ and the angels that God sent my way.

INTRODUCTION

I must admit that I sometimes struggle with the concept of holiness. However, I am convinced that the Catholic Church, as the bride of Christ, has God's divine wisdom about what it means to be holy. The purpose of this book is to gather information about holiness and present it in a simple way that is easy to comprehend. I am fascinated by our faith's rich history and doctrine and deeply passionate about Catholic Apologetics; therefore, I strive to support my writings with factual information.

I have researched and gathered relevant data on holiness for this book. I hope that it will serve as a valuable resource for those who seek to understand holiness and want to work towards achieving it in their daily lives. My goal in writing this book is to help readers better understand holiness and its importance in our lives. I hope all readers will at least take away something useful from it. I pray that this book will be a valuable tool for anyone seeking to deepen their relationship with God and cultivate a more holy life.

This book will answer some common questions about living a holy life. What does it mean to be holy? Where do we begin our pursuit of holiness? The topic of holiness is complex and can be perplexing because there are no definitive steps to follow. We cannot simply say, "Do a, b, and c, and you will become holy." It is much more intricate than that. Holiness is unique to each person. God has a specific plan for every individual, and each person grows in holiness in their own way. In a concert, every instrument is crucial to creating the perfect melody. If we miss the piano, the melody suffers; if we miss the flute or the saxophone, it will be different. Each instrument has a unique function, just as each human being has a role in life. Whether this role is big or small, every individual is an essential member of the mystical body of Christ.

INTRODUCTION

In this topic, we will create a guide consisting of 14 steps that will help us follow the path to holiness. This guide is inspired by the teachings of the Catholic Church, the exemplary lives of the Saints, the advice of the Church fathers, and other valuable resources. We hope that this guide will assist you through this challenging path.

THE PATH TO HOLINESS

A 14 STEP GUIDE TO GET IN THE RIGHT PATH

1

THE SAINTS OF THE CATHOLIC CHURCH

Before we begin our journey toward holiness, it's important to understand the process of canonizing a saint in the Catholic Church. This is because holiness is an achievable goal for each of us, and the Church takes the canonization process very seriously. A canonized saint is someone who has achieved a high level of spiritual perfection and has left behind a legacy of how to live a holy life.

WHO ARE THE SAINTS

The Saints are converted sinners who have turned away from their sinful ways and have chosen to live a life of holiness. They are now in Heaven with God and serve as an example for all to live a faith-filled life. The lives of the Saints are a testimony to God's work and serve as irrefutable proof of His promises. Even though the Saints lived in different times, they all carry the same message in harmony with the scriptures. The Saints are also our lawyers in Heaven, as they intercede for us and aid us in our spiritual battle against the powers of the evil one.

. . .

TYPE OF SAINTS

The Catholic Church recognizes two types of saints: those who have been formally canonized, such as St. Faustina and Padre Pio, and those who are everyone else in Heaven. The Church offers canonized saints for public veneration and imitation

Canonization of a Saint

In the Church, there are three steps to be canonized as Saint.

Venerable

A person who has died and is recognized by the Pope for leading a virtuous and heroic life.

Blessed

It is the second stage in the process of the declaration of Holiness. To qualify as blessed, a miracle obtained through the intercession of this candidate is required, but a miracle is not required if he is a martyr.

Saint

A Second Miracle after beatification is required to canonize a Saint.

Procedure

Every candidate must wait five years after death before the proceedings begin. The Pope has the authority to shorten this waiting period. As an example, Pope John Paul II shortened the beatification process of Mother Teresa of Calcutta by removing three years from the waiting period. Additionally, Pope Benedict XVI eliminated the entire waiting period for the procedure of his predecessor, Pope John Paul II.

Research

The bishop of the candidate's diocese is responsible for initiating the investigation. The petitioners are the faithful calling for an investigation to be opened. Once the investigation has begun, the candidate will be called a **Servant of GOD.**

Diocesan Information Process

A court will thoroughly investigate the candidate's life, including calling witnesses and examining evidence. This process can take several years.

Congregation for the Cause of Saints

After the evidence is collected, it is sent to Rome, where nine theologians will vote either for or against it. If the decision is favorable, the approval of bishops and cardinals who are members of the congregation for the cause of the saints will be sought. If everything goes according to plan, the Holy Father will authorize the congregation to issue a decree that declares the candidate Venerable or Blessed. Upon canonization, the Blessed will acquire the title of Saint.

Saints at Baptism

When we are baptized, all our sins and their consequences are erased, releasing us from all debts. Therefore, at the moment of baptism, we become saints, even if it is for a brief period before we sin again. When infants are baptized, we welcome a little saint into our homes. Since babies cannot comprehend right from wrong, they cannot commit any sins until they are old enough to understand such distinctions. The Catechism of the Church (CCC) **1263** tells us:

> " *By Baptism all sins are forgiven, original sin and all personal sins, as well as all punishment for sin.*[65] *In those who have been reborn nothing remains that would*

impede their entry into the Kingdom of God, neither Adam's sin, nor personal sin, nor the consequences of sin, the gravest of which is separation from God."[1]

Leading a pious life and practicing the sacraments are essential to regaining and maintaining holiness. Holiness is a state of being united with God, where one's thoughts, actions, and desires are aligned with God's will, and it's something that all Christians are called to achieve.

Leviticus 11:44:
"[44] For I am the Lord your God: be holy because I am holy."[2]

To be holy is to be obedient and humble.

2

ATTAINING HOLINESS

HOW CAN WE BECOME HOLY

The only way to Heaven is through obedience and humility, the two essential virtues we must possess. The Ten Commandments of God are based on these two virtues.

OBEDIENCE:

When we choose to obey, we consciously decide to relinquish control and trust in something greater than ourselves. We surrender our desires, preferences, and ideas to embrace God's will. Obedience is an act of the will.

HUMILITY:

Humility is a virtue that helps us recognize our insignificance in comparison to the greatness of God. It involves acknowledging that we can do nothing without His help. By practicing humility, we reject the temptation of the serpent's offer, "You will be like God" (Genesis 3:5) and acknowledge that we are not and will never be like God. Humility allows us to submit ourselves to God and others, recognizing that we are all made in his image. It is a powerful tool in our fight against evil.

Why do we need obedience and humility?

Let us revisit the Book of Genesis, particularly the accounts of the fall of the angels and Adam and Eve. What was the sin of Adam and Eve? It was disobedience. And what about the sin of the angels? It was pride that was used against our first parents to entice them into sin by saying, *"You will be like God."* (Gen 3:5)

How do you deal with disobedience? The answer is obedience. And how do you overcome pride? The answer is humility. We lost our unity with God through prideful disobedience; only through obedience and humility will we regain it.

For example:

In the sacrament of confession, it's important to humble ourselves before another man, a priest, by bending our knees, acknowledging our faults, and seeking guidance. Through this sacrament, we practice obedience and humility, the two most powerful weapons against evil and our best allies in our journey toward holiness. That's why Satan despises confession and priests. This is something that the Saints knew and practiced often,

Padre Pio practiced humility and obedience when his Bishop, who didn't believe in his mystical revelations, severely persecuted him.

Pope Francis wrote about Padre Pio:

> *"Charity animated by faith has the power to disarm the forces of evil. #SanPíodaPietrelcina fought against evil throughout his life **with humility, with obedience, with the cross, offering pain for love.**"*

St. John of the Cross warns that the devil tempts us with pride, especially when we become overly confident in our spirituality.

> " **The devil's bait is pride** —especially the pride that arises from spiritual presumption."

WHAT IS HOLINESS?

Holiness is returning to the original state of our first parents, Adam and Eve, before the fall. In this original state, they were in perfect communion with God, and doing His will was easy and natural. The inclination towards good was present from the beginning; however, they gave into temptation, resulting in sin entering the world.

After the fall of Adam and Eve, the tendency towards sin became part of human nature. As a result, it has become effortless for us to commit sins without much thought. Obeying God's commandments has become more challenging and almost unnatural. It demands a considerable amount of effort and sacrifice from our end. We can achieve spiritual purity and harmony with God by returning to our original state, just like our first parents before the fall.

As we progress on our journey towards holiness, we will discover that carrying out God's will become effortless, and gradually, we will lose the desire to sin. This is because our original holiness is being restored.

Holiness is not a one-time achievement but a continuous

striving toward moral perfection. It involves a constant battle of falling and getting back up again without ever giving up. We can attain holiness through our everyday lives and interactions with others. Holiness requires practicing obedience and humility and accepting and enduring suffering. The path to Heaven is not an easy one. It requires us to carry the Cross, just as Jesus did. This means we must be willing to endure hardship, suffering, and sacrifice to follow God's will.

Sanctification is a crucial part of this journey. It is the process through which God works within us to make us holy. This involves transforming our hearts and minds as we learn to love God more deeply and put his will above our own desires. Sanctification is an ongoing process. We can never claim to have achieved holiness and must always be vigilant against sin and temptation. The only fact we can affirm is that we are <u>working towards holiness</u>. He who struggles will persevere in his sanctifying journey.

How do we know if we are on the Path to Holiness?

Simply by checking our progress. Are we the same person as last year? What positive changes have we made? What sins have we conquered?

We must decide to either completely eradicate our sin or die trying. There is no such thing as stealing, hating, or swearing "less" than before. True transformation involves uprooting the source of our sins. While certain behaviors can be difficult to overcome, it is also true that we can try harder. I bet if someone offers us 1 billion dollars to quit swearing, smoking, or stealing, we will do it in a heartbeat. Hypocritical, isn't it?

One of our human weaknesses is our tendency to be presumptuous. We often make grand plans and set ambitious goals for the future, like the famous "New Year's resolutions." The reality is that **<u>we don't have time</u>**. We might be gone tonight. From the moment we are born, the clock starts ticking, and we are heading towards death. We don't know how much time we have left. The only certainty in life is that we will all die someday; nothing else is guaranteed.

Life, as we know it, is a journey that prepares us for eternity. During this journey, we are molded, shaped, and nourished with the necessary nutrients to face the true reality. Just like a baby in its mother's womb, we go through various growth stages until we are ready to be born into the world. Similarly, we must be prepared for our eternal life by nourishing our souls and being born again from the Spirit.

AS JESUS SAID:

> *"Truly, truly, I say to you, unless one is born of water and the Spirit, he cannot enter the kingdom of God. ⁶ That which is born of the flesh is flesh, and that which is born of the Spirit is spirit.*[a]*john 3:5-6*[1]

The decision to reject sin and become a better version of ourselves must be made today because the future is not guaranteed. Do it now.

THE STAGES OF HOLINESS

According to theologians and doctors of the church, spiritual life can be divided into three stages: purgative, illuminative, and unitive. This three-stage model is often compared to the stages of human life, with childhood representing the Purgative Way, adolescence representing the Illuminative Way, and adulthood representing the Unitive Way.

. . .

IN THE PURGATIVE STATE, the soul feels an intense desire to connect with God and decides to follow His ways. However, it struggles to overcome the temptations. During this stage, the soul moves away from sinful ways, distancing itself from committing mortal sins. In the quest to draw closer to God, the individual forms the habit of prayer and practices piety, seeking to strengthen their relationship with Him.

DURING THE ILLUMINATIVE STAGE, the soul gains spiritual strength and experiences a significant transformation in daily life. The soul grows in virtue and rejects anything that does not align with God's will. In this state, the soul is tested by trials and tribulations but also enjoys consolations and blessings. The soul has better control over its actions and avoids committing venial sins.

THE UNITIVE STAGE is a profound and intimate union with God.
During this stage, the soul becomes more passive while God becomes more active. The soul is no longer afraid of fears and sufferings because it recognizes them as instruments of salvation and closeness to the Creator. The soul seeks to unite itself with God as much as possible and yearns for Him with a profound thirst. The soul's love for God becomes all-consuming, and it finds joy in constant prayer, which brings it closer to Him.

TO BE "GOOD" IS NOT THE SAME AS BEING HOLY.

We often hear people say, "I'm a good person. I haven't killed anyone, so I should go straight to Heaven." They justify their claim by pointing out that they have not committed any heinous crimes or caused any harm to others. However, it is important to remember that every human being carries the divine breath of goodness within them, known as the Spirit of God. This spirit is present within us from the moment of conception, an inherent goodness that is an integral part of human nature. This divine breath imbues every individual with a sense of purpose and morality, and it is a testament to our remarkable potential. We see this in Genesis 2:7:

> "⁷ then the Lord God formed man of dust from the ground, **and breathed into his nostrils the breath of life**; and man became a living being."

The fact is that it is not enough to be "good." We must change from within our souls. In its natural state, our soul is not good enough to enter Heaven. Merely loving animals or being kind to people who are kind to us is not sufficient. If we pass away in our natural state, we will not be able to enter Heaven directly. We must attain the supernatural state, which is the state of Heaven. On earth, we prepare ourselves in our natural state to reach the supernatural state and attain sanctifying grace.

3

THE GRACE OF GOD

SANCTIFYING GRACE

God infuses a supernatural gift of mercy and grace into our souls at baptism and drives us to holiness and worship. We activate sanctifying grace by choosing God and doing his will. With sanctifying grace, we rise from our natural state and participate in the divine nature. However, we can lose this grace with mortal sin, and we can regain it through sacramental confession. It is only through sanctifying grace that we can reach heaven.

> "*²³ Jesus answered and said to him: If any one love me, he will keep my word, and my Father will love him, **and we will come to him, and will make our abode with him.**" (John 14:23)

THE PATH TO HOLINESS

Catechism of the Catholic Church CCC **2023**:

 2023. "Sanctifying grace is the gratuitous gift of his life that God makes to us; it is infused by the Holy Spirit into the soul to heal it of sin and to sanctify it."[1]

ACTUAL GRACE

IT IS a divine assistance that God provides to human beings to help them achieve eternal salvation. This grace is granted through the merits of Jesus Christ and makes us "good" in the eyes of the world. Actual grace is bestowed upon us at the right time so that we can perform well in our daily lives. It enables us to make good decisions, endure evil, show love, and perform good deeds.

For instance, it's possible for a serial killer to have a loving relationship with his mother and be respected in his community. Equally, a thief may have the capacity to help others in need. It's also possible for someone to hate and discriminate while feeling compassion for specific individuals or animals.

Infamous Pablo Escobar, who was involved in drug trafficking, did assist many families and sick people. Surprisingly, he even established a neighborhood of 250 homes for low-income families. However, despite being a loving father, he was a violent and heartless murderer. His love for his family ended up leading to his downfall. By Actual grace, he could experience feelings of compassion and kindness and be "good" to some. However, this is not enough to get straight to Heaven. In other words,

 We can't go to heaven by being who we are but by who we become

In hell, for example, the soul no longer experiences the actual grace, which is why the soul in hell is only capable of feeling hatred, not love.

* * *

4

THE ENEMIES OF HOLINESS

THE SEVEN DEADLY SINS

Our human nature is inherently flawed and inclined towards certain sinful behaviors, called Deadly Sins or Capital Sins. They are named as such because they serve as a foundation for other sins to develop, much like cities and neighborhoods spring up from the capital city of a country. These seven **sins** are each led by a particular fallen angel, a prince of hell, and they are often joined by other sins, leading to a dangerous chain reaction of sin in the soul. This domino effect can cause a legion of sins to accumulate and grow, creating a heavy burden for the individual.

Angels are organized in hierarchies based on their rank and authority. The higher-ranking angels wield more power and authority over the lower-ranking ones. However, when certain angels rebelled against God, they were cast out of Heaven and maintained their hierarchy in Hell. In this fallen state, each demon represents a specific sin. The more severe the sin, the higher the rank of the demon representing it. These demons are organized into a hierarchy similar to the angelic realm, with the most powerful demons at the top of the chain.

As cancer cells develop and spread throughout the body, sins can grow and take over our souls. Each sin is a demon that latches onto us and refuses to let go. The progression of sin is gradual and insidious, much like the growth of cancer. At first, we may not even notice its presence, but as time goes on, we become more and more consumed by our vices Therefore, it is imperative to fight against these sins, as they pose a direct threat to the Ten Commandments. Only through sacramental confession can they be eliminated, allowing the individual to reset and return to the path of holiness.

SAINT THOMAS AQUINAS in Summa Theologica II-II: 153:4:

 "A capital vice is one which has an excessively desirable end, so that in his desire, a man commits many sins, all of which are said to originate in that vice as their chief source."[1]

The seven deadly sins are:
Pride, Greed, Lust, Anger, Gluttony, Envy and Sloth.
We fight these sins with the seven virtues of the Holy Spirit:

1. Pride-Humility
2. Greed-generosity
3. Lust- Chastity
4. Anger-Patience
5. Gluttony-Temperance
6. Envy-Charity
7. Laziness- Diligence

* * *

5

UNDERSTANDING GOD'S WILL

Understanding God's will is a fundamental aspect of the path toward holiness, as every Saint throughout history has realized. We cannot enter the kingdom without aligning our will with God's. In fact, every creature in Heaven, Hell, and Purgatory aligns their will with God's, which underlines the importance of accepting His will completely. Those who have not learned to accept God's will in the body will inevitably learn to do so outside of it.

At the moment of death, the soul automatically accepts and unites with God's will, regardless of whether it goes to Heaven, Hell, or Purgatory. Therefore, striving to align our will with God throughout our lives is crucial to ensure our place in Heaven.

The concept of God's will tells us that He is in complete control of everything that happens in the universe. It means that nothing occurs without God's knowledge and permission. It all happens with God's will, whether a significant event or a minor occurrence.

However, when it comes to unfortunate events like wars, diseases, and suffering, people often question why God punishes us. It is essential to understand that God does not send us these evils. Instead,

 He allows them to happen because justice requires it as a consequence of our actions.

God created humans with free will, meaning we can make our own choices. We have the power to act according to God's will or in opposition to it. Unfortunately, when we turn away from God and act in ways that do not align with His will, we create the conditions for misfortunes to occur.

Allowing something does not mean interfering with our free will. Instead, it means that God respects our choices, even when not aligned with His will. In His infinite wisdom, God knows that allowing us to experience the consequences of our choices can help us grow and learn valuable lessons.

Our words alone are not enough to express our desires to Him. He looks at our actions and the intentions of our hearts. We must learn from trials and tribulations and grow stronger in our faith. Only then can we receive the blessings God has in store for us.

LET'S read Psalm 37:4:

> *" Take delight in the Lord,*
> *and he will give you the **desires of your heart**.."*

It is important to acknowledge that indulging in sinful activities like stealing, fornicating, or holding grudges can have severe repercussions. Our actions have consequences, and the negative impact of our misdeeds will catch up with us sooner or later.

. . .

ROMANS 6:23:

 ²³ For the **wages of sin is death**. But the grace of God, life everlasting, in Christ Jesus our Lord."

IN THIS SCENARIO, let's imagine that we are walking with our best friend on a rainy day. My best friend owns the umbrella, so I am safe and dry under it. However, what would happen if I insulted and rejected my friend? He would leave and take his umbrella, leaving me exposed and vulnerable to the rain.

Similarly, God protects us from evil but does not force Himself upon us. If we reject Him, He will take what belongs to Him, allowing us to face our sins' consequences. Is my friend responsible for me being exposed to the rain? Is God responsible for our misfortunes? These are important questions to consider.

GOD IN CONTROL

Everything is under God's control; there is nothing He doesn't know or allow.

MATTHEW 10:29-30 TELLS US:

> *"Are not two sparrows sold for a penny? Yet not one of them will fall to the ground apart from your Father. ³⁰ **And even the hairs of your head are all counted**. ³¹ So do not be afraid; you are of more value than many sparrows."*

EVERY EVENT AND EVERY POSITION, whether political or job-related, has been allowed by God. A restaurant manager is a manager because God has allowed it, and the president of a nation is president because God allowed it. God also allows our ability to move our legs, speak, smell, and laugh. We are alive this morning, even though many died last night because God allowed us to live. Whether we are healthy or sick, God allows our health status. Even the smallest things that happen are permitted by God's will.

If we were to sum it all up in one sentence, we would say:

 "We can't even fart without the will of God."

This Bible passage says it all:

> [5] *I am the vine: you the branches: he that abideth in me, and I in him, the same beareth much fruit: for **without me you can do nothing.**" John 15:5*

Did he say, "Without me, can you do 50%? 10%? A little bit?" No, right? It says **NOTHING**, and nothing means zero, nada.

Saints Against the Pope?

It is a heresy to pretend that God is not in control or to believe that something is happening without His will. Let us take the example of our current Pope, often criticized by many. It is important to remember that God put him in that position, and nothing happens without His will. Who are we to reject God's will? It is a sin to speak ill of our brothers and sisters, especially the Holy Father. While respectful criticism is acceptable, it should exclude sarcasm and hatred. We should pray for the Pope and never go against him or support malicious criticism. It is important to remember that no Saint has ever been against the Pope, despite having some bad Popes in history.

We often hear comments such as "He shouldn't have been

Pope," "We have the wrong Pope," or "The antichrist Pope." What does this mean? Are we saying that God was wrong? Are we implying that God was watching us humans choose this Pope while shaking His head in disagreement helplessly? This is a heresy, as it suggests that God is not omnipotent and that humans have some power outside of His power.

We must not forget that God's ways are beyond our comprehension, and we must not try to question His decisions or reject His will. Instead, we must have faith in God and pray for a better outcome and the well-being of our brothers and sisters, including the Holy Father.

OUR WILL IS UNITED with God's will.

After leaving behind the physical body, the soul gains a remarkable understanding of who God is and His plan for salvation. The soul willingly aligns its will with the will of God. The soul is aware of the purpose for which it was born and the reason for its existence. The soul comprehends why God allowed it to die, the times God called it to holiness, and how it responded to His call. The soul also knows whether it is worthy of God's presence and where it should go by justice.

In God's presence, no soul is concerned about its earthly affairs. The soul does not ask, "Lord, who will care for my children? They need me." "I left many debts." Instead, the soul is fully aware that God is in control of everything and willingly accepts His will.

Many people don't accept God's will, either out of ignorance or convenience. They want to control their future by removing God from the picture and instead relying on heresies like tarot cards and mediums. Let's analyze one of these readings we found online:

In this scenario, a medium claimed to have conveyed a message from a woman's deceased grandmother. According to the woman, it was the first time she had communicated with her grandmother after her passing. We can assume that Grandma is saved and is now residing in heaven, basking in the glory of God, surrounded by angels, and experiencing indescribable wonders in her new heavenly home. What happens when we see something close to those wonders? Something so important and profound? We'll probably run and tell everybody.

The message conveyed by the medium also contains a rather unusual comment from the grandmother about how lovely she looks in the photograph that the woman gave to the medium, followed by a reference to her false teeth. Let us analyze this in detail.:

If we were to pass away and find ourselves in the presence of Jesus and the patriarchs, it's hard to imagine the overwhelming emotions we would feel. With only one chance to communicate with a loved one, we would likely be filled with a sense of urgency to share our experience and offer guidance. Would we ask our loved ones how our teeth look, or would we be compelled to tell them about seeing Jesus for the first time and reassure them that Heaven is real?

The so-called grandmother makes no mention of God or His glory. Instead, her final advice is to "Love you and honor you" (not God) and "put your pains in a suitcase" and offer them to her (grandma). It sounds like a script straight out of the Three Stooges show and unfortunately, people fall for these lies. Many mediums have deceived thousands of fools. Such are the messages of these scammers, who have nothing to do with God or His plan of salvation.

* * *

14 STEPS TO HOLINESS

6

STEP ONE

THE SURRENDER OF THE FREE WILL

As we embark on the path of holiness, we must make a profound and conscious decision to choose God and collaborate with His plan for humanity. This decision requires us to use our free will to choose between our own desires and God's will; that is the only way to reach perfection in the pursuit of holiness. It is important to note that we should not assume that God already knows everything and, therefore, we don't need to ask Him for anything. Rather, we should exercise our free will to allow God to act in our lives, just as Mary did when she said YES at the Annunciation.

When we accept the will of God, we may not always have a complete understanding of it. However, this does not prevent us from accepting it with open hearts. We can have faith in His plan and trust that our understanding will come in due time. For instance, Mary did not understand how she could be pregnant while still being a virgin. She asked, *"How shall this be done, because I know not man?"* (Luke 1:34). Nonetheless, she gave her free will to God and trusted Him.

Some individuals might not fully comprehend the concept of the Trinity, but they can accept it because it is Church doctrine. With God's grace, understanding of this concept will come later. This is an example of accepting God's will. When we give Him our free will, God will reveal Himself to us uniquely and personally.

LET'S READ St. Faustina's diary #699.

> "My daughter, tell the whole world about My inconceivable mercy. I desire that the Feast of Mercy be a refuge and shelter for all souls, and especially for poor sinners. I pour out a whole ocean of graces upon those souls **who approach** the fount of My mercy "[1]

IN THIS STATEMENT, Jesus emphasizes the need for souls to approach Him. He doesn't imply that He already knows everything and that He will bestow His grace upon everyone whether they desire it or not. We must use our free will and willingly seek Him out so that He can work within us.

Let's examine the case of a former Satanist Zachary King [2] who converted to Catholicism after a mystical experience. Before his experience, he unknowingly said "Yes" to God twice:

ONE DAY, Zachary, a satanic worshiper, and his friends were at an abortion clinic performing satanic rituals.

They overheard a group of Catholics praying the rosary outside the clinic. His friends encouraged him to listen and repeat the words they were saying.

Zachary hesitated but ultimately repeated the words as instructed, though his heart wasn't in it.

> "Hail Mary, full of grace..."

ZACHARY FOUND HIMSELF PRAYING UNWILLINGLY, using his free will for reasons unrelated to the purpose of prayer. However, fate intervened when a lady approached him at work in a jewelry store and offered him a miraculous medal of the Virgin Mary. Despite his initial hesitation, Zachary accepted the gift, and as soon as the medal touched his hand, he had a profound and mystical experience with the Virgin Mary. This life-changing event transformed Zachary's life, and he began preaching his testimony and working tirelessly against the evils of abortion and Satanism in the United States.

THIS IS an excellent example of how utilizing our free will can attract God's blessings without comprehending it entirely. Zachary strongly disliked the Church and God; however, Zachary's actions contradicted his feelings. He relinquished his free will twice - first when he recited the Hail Mary, and second when he accepted the sacramental medal. Likewise, when we indulge in occultism or engage in new-age spirituality, such as practicing yoga or using seemingly harmless amulets, we unknowingly subject ourselves to danger. Our free will is a sacred gift, and we must exercise caution when making choices, for they carry significant consequences.

In one of the meetings between Jesus and St. Faustina, the Lord asked her to love her enemies, which was a difficult request for St. Faustina. She admitted that she could not find any love in her heart for them. He explained that even if she felt uncomfortable or negative towards her enemies, she should still want to forgive and pray for them. In other words, Jesus was teaching St. Faustina that it is not necessary to wait to feel love for those who have wronged us. Instead, we can love them simply by choosing to do so, exercising our free will.

Jesus taught her that we should aim for the desire to love, even if we don't feel like it. The feelings will come later by grace. Love and forgiveness are acts of the will. We can choose to love or forgive even if we don't feel it.

LET'S read the Diary of St. Faustina 1628:

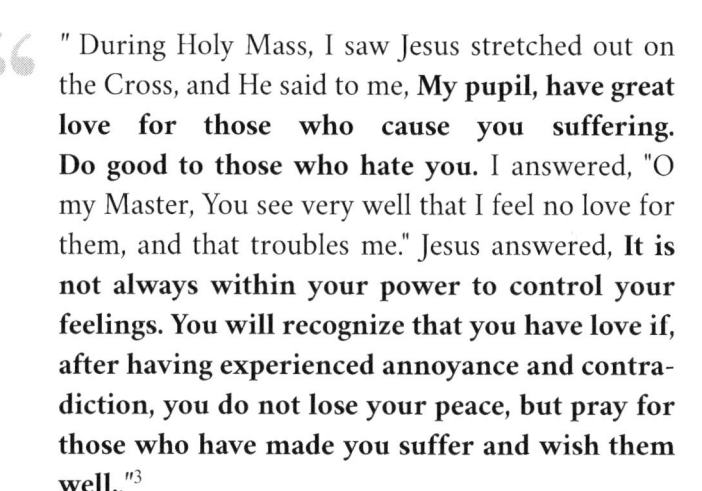

> " During Holy Mass, I saw Jesus stretched out on the Cross, and He said to me, **My pupil, have great love for those who cause you suffering. Do good to those who hate you.** I answered, "O my Master, You see very well that I feel no love for them, and that troubles me." Jesus answered, **It is not always within your power to control your feelings. You will recognize that you have love if, after having experienced annoyance and contradiction, you do not lose your peace, but pray for those who have made you suffer and wish them well..**"[3]

Let's begin the first step by submitting our free will to God.:

> "Lord, I give you my free will so that your WILL be done and not mine."

ASKING FOR HOLINESS

In today's world, the desire to be holy is often considered scandalous or laughable. Our inherently sinful nature causes us to reject the pursuit of holiness. When we read about the lives of the Saints, it can feel like we are reading about aliens from another planet; that's how deceived we have become. It is important to remember that being holy means not conforming to the ways of this world, as stated in John 17:14.

> *"I have given them thy word; and the world has hated them because they are not of the world, even as I am not of the world. "*

WE ASK GOD FOR HOLINESS, a grace that can only be attained with His help through sanctifying grace.

> *"...for without me you can do nothing."*
> John 15:5

ASKING God to make us holy is a daring request. When we reflect upon the lives of the Saints of the Church and the gruesome ways in which many of them were martyred, we are reminded of the difficulty of the path toward holiness. Pursuing such an arduous path requires great strength and bravery, as it may involve enduring great hardship and suffering. Choosing not to pursue holiness may seem easier; only a courageous heart can do it.

We can pray to God from anywhere as He is omnipresent, but the best place to do so is during the Holy Mass. It is a sacred ceremony that brings together the three Churches - militant, suffering, and triumphant - and the divine beings such as the Angels, the Saints, our mother, and the sacrificial lamb. It is at this holy place where we consume the actual Body and Blood of Jesus that we gather the courage to ask Him for the gift of holiness.

" *Lord, I want to be holy; help me...*

BY SURRENDERING our free will to God and His Church, we humble ourselves and take the first step toward holiness.

* * *

AGREEMENT

Date:

Today, I went to mass at:_____ And I asked God for the gift of holiness.

Signature _____

7

STEP TWO

SACRAMENTAL CONFESSION

As we decide to pursue holiness and follow God, we must first free ourselves from the chains that bind us to Satan. These chains are the sins that have taken root in our lives and hinder our relationship with God. We must begin with a soul that is clean and willing to receive His grace. Therefore, preparing our souls by sacramentally confessing our sins is essential. This means purging ourselves of all transgressions, particularly mortal sin and rekindling our friendship with God. In doing so, our soul becomes a worthy dwelling for God's presence.

MORTAL SIN

The term "mortal" is derived from the Latin word "Mors," which means "death." A mortal sin is a grave sin that kills the soul, completely separating us from God. A person with mortal sin is a dead man walking. They are spiritually dead, and their soul is in a state of separation from God. A soul with mortal sin is already positioned in Hell, even if the person is still alive.

Should the person die at that moment, they would go straight to Hell.

Living in mortal sin is like playing a deadly game of russian roulette. Every time we commit a mortal sin, we put our souls at risk of eternal damnation. Mortal sin can invite demonic possession as it creates a friendship with the demonic by killing our friendship with God, putting us under Satan's authority. To regain life for our souls and rekindle our friendship with God, we must confess sacramentally as soon as possible.

HOW DO WE CONFESS OUR SINS?

Before confessing our sins, it is crucial to undertake a comprehensive examination of our conscience. This involves identifying our transgressions and acknowledging our shortcomings. In doing so, we cultivate a contrite heart, recognizing the gravity of our sinful state and the need to make amends.

It is imperative that we confess all our sins, no matter how small or seemingly insignificant they may be. Concealing any wrongdoing will only impede our spiritual growth and prevent us from achieving true repentance and forgiveness. By acknowledging and confessing our transgressions, we can move forward with a clean conscience and a renewed commitment to living a virtuous life.

> "Unconfessed sin is unforgiven sin."

What about sins we don't remember?

It is important to confess both past and present sins, seeking God's help to remember all wrongdoings from the first time we become aware of right and wrong. We can do this by asking for the grace of the Holy Spirit. Writing down our sins can also help us recall them. Every past sin, whether considered a grave or minor offense, must be confessed, and we must make reparations for each of them.

EXAMPLE:

Marleen, who is 62, suddenly remembered an event from her childhood when she pushed a boy off the stairs. Feeling guilty about it, Marleen confessed this sin in her next confession. To make amends, Marleen has decided to fast and pray the rosary for that child, all the bullies in the world, and their victims.

> Either we repair our sins here on earth, or we repair them in purgatory (if saved)

HOW OFTEN SHOULD WE GO TO CONFESSION?

The Catholic Church mandates that the faithful confess their sins at least once a year, as mentioned in the Catechism (CCC 1457). However, to remain in a state of grace, it is advisable to confess more frequently. Ideally, one should confess once a week, but at a minimum, confessing once a month is recommended. Many Saints regularly followed this practice. For instance, Mother Teresa of Calcutta confessed her sins once a week, even though it was evident that she didn't commit mortal sins every week. In the same way, Pope John Paul II also went to confession once a week, demonstrating the importance of this sacrament in the Catholic faith. Padre Pio spoke about the importance of confession.

> "Even if the room is closed, it needs to be cleaned every week."

Venial Sins Are Also Dangerous

Venial sins are often considered minor and insignificant,

but their potential impact on our lives should not be ignored. These seemingly minor transgressions can lead to more serious sins if left unconfessed. Venial sins prepare our souls for the reception of mortal sins. Venial sins are deceiving because they look harmless; in reality, they are like pregnant cockroaches breeding evil. Therefore, it is crucial to confess them sacramentally to ensure that we keep our sins under control.

St. Faustina wrote:

Diary #1016

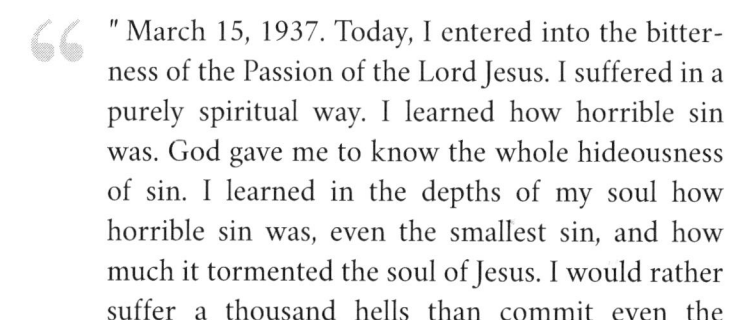

> " March 15, 1937. Today, I entered into the bitterness of the Passion of the Lord Jesus. I suffered in a purely spiritual way. I learned how horrible sin was. God gave me to know the whole hideousness of sin. I learned in the depths of my soul how horrible sin was, even the smallest sin, and how much it tormented the soul of Jesus. I would rather suffer a thousand hells than commit even the **smallest venial sin."**[1]

St. Teresa of Avila tells us:

> " Keep this in mind, for it is very important advice, so do not neglect it until you find you have such a fixed determination not to offend the Lord that you would rather lose a thousand lives and be persecuted by the whole world, than commit one mortal sin, **and until you are most careful not to commit venial sins.;**"

> " From any sin, however small, committed with full knowledge, may God deliver us, it"[2]

Frequency:

We must strive to keep our souls free from sin on our path to holiness. We should practice confession at least once a week, if not once a month.

* * *

AGREEMENT

Date:

Today, I went to confession, and from now on, I commit to practicing confession every:

☐ Week
   ☐ Month
   Or every _____ month

Signature: _____

8

STEP THREE

REPARATIONS FOR OUR SINS

Every sin that we commit has consequences and demands reparation. This debt must be paid because justice demands it. If we fail to pay it in this life, we will have to pay it after death in purgatory.

WHAT IS PURGATORY

Those who die and attain salvation but do not achieve holiness must be purged of their imperfections and sinful attachments before joining the other Saints in heaven. Purgatory is necessary to complete in our souls any work of sanctification that we have not completed during our lifetime. The Church has referred to this purge as a purifying or refining fire that burns sin from our souls. Purgatory is not a third option for the soul. Rather, we are either saved or not. We either go to Heaven or Hell. In Purgatory, every soul has attained salvation. The souls in Purgatory cannot sin, and their will is perfectly aligned with the will of God. Like in Hell, the greatest pain of the souls in Purgatory is their separation from God. However, unlike in Hell, these souls have peace because they know that they will see God one day.

Matthew 5:24-25

> ^{25} Come to terms quickly with your accuser while you are on the way to court[k] with him, or your accuser may hand you over to the judge, and the judge to the guard, and you will be thrown **into prison**. ^{26} Truly I tell you, you will never get out **until you have paid the last penny.**

THE IMPORTANCE OF REPARATIONS FOR SINS

As humans, we tend to avoid pain - it's natural. When we suffer, we can make amends for our sins and the sins of the world. Suffering is not infertile; it can bear abundant fruits when accepted with love. Nothing goes to waste in God's eyes. That is why the Church encourages us to observe fasting, penance, and mortification days. These acts of reparation help us make up for the consequences of sin and shorten the time spent in purgatory.

We make reparations by obeying God, offering prayers, fasting, and doing works of charity. The best way to repair sin is to fix the situation immediately. For example:

Joe stole a wallet from a store. He decides to confess his mistake during his next visit to church. He returned what he stole and taught his children the importance of honesty.

Elena had an abortion; she has since confessed and feels remorse for her actions. To fight against abortion, she has joined pro-life groups and offers prayers and masses for those who practice abortions and the doctors who perform them.

Elena also discusses the harmful effects and consequences of abortion with her friends to raise awareness.

The Virgin Mary to the Little Shepherds of Fatima:

> " **Sacrifice yourselves for sinners**, and say many times, especially whenever you make some sacrifice: O Jesus, it is for love of You, for the conversion of sinners, and **in reparation for the sins** committed against the Immaculate Heart of Mary."[1]

The angel who appeared in the Fatima apparitions instructed the visionaries:

> "Offer up everything in your power as a sacrifice to the Lord **in reparation** for the sins by which He is offended, and in supplication for the conversion of sinners . . . More than all else, accept and bear with resignation the sufferings that God may send you.'."[2]

And taught them this prayer:

> "Most Holy Trinity, Father, Son, and Holy Ghost, I adore Thee profoundly and offer Thee the most precious Body, Blood, Soul, and Divinity of Jesus Christ, present in all the tabernacles of the earth, **in reparation** for the insults, sacrileges, and indifference with which He is offended. And through the infinite merits of His Most Sacred Heart and of the Immaculate Heart of Mary, I beg Thee for the conversion of poor sinners."[3]

. . .

"The failure to make reparations for ourselves and humanity is a sin of omission."

How Long Can We Make Reparation for Sins?

Repairing a sin is an ongoing process. It is difficult to determine if we have effectively made amends for our sins. The consequences of sin can have a lasting impact and can cause a domino effect that only God knows the extent of.

It's difficult to determine exactly when a sin has been fully resolved, how long it lasted, and the damage it caused. One way to alleviate the consequences of sin is through indulgences, if they are accepted at all. Unfortunately, we won't know this until the end of our lives, but it is one of the best options to make amends for our debts. That is why indulgences have always been very popular, especially in the Middle Ages.

Frequency:

When we remember a sin, we need to make amends immediately. We can ask God to use our prayers, offerings, and charitable works to repair the harm caused by that sin. Making reparations involves several acts of piety. Although we may not know for certain whether our sin has been fully repaired, we can trust in the divine mercy that it has.

* * *

AGREEMENT

Date:

Today, I began to repair my sins, starting with the sin of:
_____

Signature: _____

9

STEP FOUR

DETACHMENT FROM WORLDLY THINGS

1 Timothy 6:6-7
"⁶ But godliness with contentment is great gain.
⁷ For we brought nothing into this world: and certainly we can carry nothing out."[1]

Now that we have purified our inner selves, it is equally important to cleanse our external environment. This involves cleaning our homes and removing any pagan objects that do not align with God's teachings. Such objects include esoteric books, feng shui practices, amulets, and superstitious artifacts from other religions, such as Buddha statues, Turkish eyes, and dream catchers.

Any jewelry that features a pagan design, or new-age material must be removed. We should refrain from superstitious practices such as believing that broken glass brings bad luck, the purse on the floor causes money to go away, and that horoscopes and lucky charms have any real effect.

Any act of pagan worship or the presence of superstitious objects can act as a gateway for evil forces to enter our homes. These practices are said to create portals through which malevolent entities can enter our world. Therefore, it is suggested that we should rid ourselves of such practices and objects to maintain a safe and peaceful environment within our homes. It is essential to lead a simple life free from unnecessary materialism. We do not need to accumulate an abundance of clothes or shoes. If we reflect on the lives of the Saints, we can see that they lived modestly, with little to no extravagance. They never indulged in opulence or hoarded worldly possessions. We must strive to lead a simple, humble, and minimalistic life to follow their example.

PRACTICING THE CUSTODY OF THE SENSES

The Custody of the Senses refers to the act of consciously guarding our senses from being lured into temptation. Our senses serve as the portals through which our soul and mind perceive the world around us. By being vigilant and cautious about what we allow into our senses, we can protect ourselves from negative influences and maintain the purity and focus of our souls.

> Oh! how many are lost by indulging their sight! – St. Alphonsus de Ligouri[2]

> *29 If your right eye causes you to sin, tear it out and throw it away;. Matthew 5:29*

Custody of the Eyes

We should refrain from looking at people with lust, which can lead us to sin.

It is of utmost importance to be conscious of the content we consume and support on social media. We must strive to avoid any material that offends God, such as films, shows, or music that promotes immorality or ungodly values.

In addition, we should be aware of the content we read, such as magazines, articles, or books, that contradicts our religious beliefs. Certain content, especially pornographic or violent material, can be harmful to our spiritual well-being. We must also refrain from supporting pagan, profane, or heretical videos and only support content that aligns with the will of God.

Many movies nowadays contain explicit sexual content. We see full-on sexual acts in most movies. How is that relevant to the story? Why do we have to witness people fornicating on TV? When I was a kid, I wasn't even allowed to watch people kissing in movies. Someone would always cover my eyes until the scene was over. What's even more disturbing is that people seem to be indifferent to this trend. The normalization of such explicit content is alarming. Movies with pornographic material win awards, and yet, we seem to turn a blind eye to the impact they have on our children. The only award they deserve is the award of fornicators.

In the present day, with the advent of digital media and instant access to information, it is all too common for individuals to become idle spectators of news and social media. We are continuously exposed to stories of individuals facing perilous situations, unfortunate incidents, and even tragic deaths from across the globe, all with a simple click of a button. We often forget that as consumers, we have a great responsibility towards others. By learning about these misfortunes, we become accountable before God for the well-being of those affected. We might think that because they are strangers, they are not our problem, but they are. The justice of God demands that we do not turn a blind eye to their pain but instead offer our prayers and, if we can, our support.

. . .

However, it is unfortunate that our response to such tragic news is often short-lived. We may offer a brief thought of sympathy, "Oh my God," or "poor thing," before moving on to the next story and laughing with the next publication, quickly forgetting the people who were suffering and needing our help.

Social media and other forms of media have turned our hearts into stone. People are reduced to mere figures on a screen, and their struggles become nothing more than a form of entertainment. It is as if we are spectators at a Roman Colosseum, watching people fight for their lives against lions, only to return to our comfortable homes, completely detached from the reality of their struggles. Be aware this is a sin of omission. It's better to turn off the news or your cell phone if you don't want to be responsible for these people. Otherwise, it's our duty to pray for each one of them. We will be held accountable before God for the actions we omit and the things our eyes ignore.

As Catholics, we have been entrusted with tools to collaborate with God's plan for salvation, and we will be liable for not making the most of those valuable tools.

Waking up

It seems that Satan is using media to eliminate the presence of God from our lives, but we may not even realize it. For instance, let's take the popular comic book hero "Superman."

He is the world's savior. He fights evil and rescues people and animals. Anyone who is in trouble calls him. His amazing stories have been a part of our childhood, and our children continue to admire this character. However, there is an underlying message in the story that suggests that we don't need God. We can do anything ourselves. Sounds familiar? "You'll be like God" (Gen 3:5).

What if Superman kneels and asks God for help before confronting evil? What if he practices the sacraments and shows that he is only an instrument of God? How would this affect our children's perception of the world? Why don't we see this version of Superheroes?

Some may argue that we exaggerate; this is a fictional story. However, it is indeed a fantasy narrative that cleverly conveys a message of self-sufficiency. It can be viewed as a form of indoctrination through entertainment. Consider this: which teenager would be more inclined to turn to tarot cards to seek insights into their future? The one who grew up with stories of superheroes who can achieve anything and rely on no higher power, or the one who grew up with stories of superheroes who depend on God for everything? The answer becomes quite evident upon reflection. The main questions are: What is happening to us? Why do we allow them to replace God? And, most importantly, when will we take action?

CUSTODY of the Ear

In today's world, it is crucial to be mindful of the type of music we listen to. We should steer clear of songs that denigrate people, contain crude sexual content, and speak ill of the Church or God. Additionally, it is advisable to avoid tunes that support abortion or new-age beliefs.

Unfortunately, we are witnessing a concerning trend where people are performing obscene dances that imitate sexual acts. Even more disturbing, children are participating in these dances and sharing videos of themselves twerking on social media. Is this the kind of legacy we want for our children? It is not even appropriate to describe this behavior as animalistic since not even animals behave in such a manner.

Furthermore, it is important to avoid listening to other people's conversations or engaging in gossip. We should pay close attention to the lyrics of the songs we listen to and ensure they are consistent with our principles. It's an excellent time to support Catholic musicians and artists who create content that is in line with our beliefs.

RESCUING LYRICS:

The trend of profaning sacred content like the Eucharist and worship songs is becoming more prevalent. We see this in social media and TV ads where actors dressed as priests behave inappropriately. Similarly, when people listen to worship music, they often cringe, but when the tune changes to secular music, they become pleased. This sends a message that worship music is boring and outdated. It's unfortunate that our sacred content is being disrespected in this way all the time; however, we can fight back and change that.

We can take some content from secular songs and repurpose it to worship God. "profaning" secular music if you will. The value of the lyrics lies in the meaning we attribute to them. For instance, if I tell a man 'I desire you,' my mind will automatically think of sexual desire, but if I say 'I desire you' to God, my mind will focus on worship. As someone with a Spanish background, I often use secular Spanish songs to worship God. For example, I can sing about how much it would hurt to leave Jesus and how much I need Him in my life, using the lyrics from the popular song 'El amor de mi vida" by Camilo Sesto. Let's take a look:

> "It hurts me more to leave you
> than to stop living...
> It would be useless to try to escape
> Because wherever I go I take you inside me
> The love of my life has been you
> My world was blind until I found your light...

THIS SONG WAS DEDICATED to all lovers back in the 1970s and 1980s. Why can't we dedicate it to Jesus? Isn't he our true love?

ANOTHER SONG I personally use to sing to Mary is a Spanish salsa song by Tito Nieves called 'El amor mas Bonito' (The Most Beautiful Love):

> *",,,You are the gift of God, who has sent me*
> *So that my voice never goes out*
> *You are for me, for me*
> *The favorite woman, the one who makes me live"*

Everybody dedicated this song to their favorite woman back in the day—their wives, their mistresses, etc. Why can't we dedicate these lyrics to our mother? Isn't she our favorite woman?

CUSTODY **of the Tongue**

It's important to avoid overeating and wasting food. Just because a plate is served doesn't mean we must finish it. Our brains take about 20 to 30 minutes to register the feeling of fullness, so it's best to stop eating when we feel satisfied.

Alcohol consumption is a common aspect of social gatherings and celebrations, but it's important to exercise moderation to avoid any potential negative consequences. While we don't want to demonize alcohol, it's crucial to maintain control over our senses and actions. The "rule of three" is a helpful guideline for responsible drinking: "The Holy Spirit leaves on the third drink." This saying is a reminder that after consuming three drinks, we may begin to lose our inhibitions and become more vulnerable to making poor decisions. This is because alcohol weakens both the flesh and the spirit and can impair judgment and decision-making abilities.

It is equally important to be mindful of our comments on social media, as we can easily commit the sin of scandal and offend others with negative opinions and attacks. Therefore, if we make comments, they must be respectful and considerate, or it would be best not to make any comments. We should always bear in mind that we will be accountable before God for every offensive word that comes out of our mouths, and we should conduct ourselves accordingly.

Custody of Smell

It is of utmost importance that we avoid using drugs and other harmful substances. In addition, we must be mindful to avoid using superstitious incense, such as sage or other types of incense, that are believed to have the power to "cleanse the energy." Whatever we use must not have any superstitious context attached to it. By doing so, we can take the necessary steps to safeguard ourselves and our surroundings from dangerous and unnecessary effects.

Custody of Tact

Certain behaviors, such as masturbation, can hinder the possibility of reproduction, which is considered an essential aspect of God's plan for human life. Therefore, it is recommended that such practices be avoided.

Moreover, it is crucial to avoid any form of aggression towards others. Theft is also deemed a morally incorrect act that violates the principles of honesty and respect for other people's property.

Let's read **Mark 9:43-47**

> "⁴³ If your hand causes you to stumble, **cut it off**; it is better for you to enter life maimed than to have two hands and to go to hell,[a] to the unquenchable fire. [b] ⁴⁵ And if your foot causes you to stumble, **cut it off**; it is better for you to enter life lame than to have two feet and to be thrown into hell.[c][d] ⁴⁷ And if your eye causes you to stumble, tear it out; it is better for you to enter the kingdom of God with one eye than to have two eyes and to be thrown into hell,"

FREQUENCY:

We must constantly guard our senses and remove all obstacles in our path to holiness.

* * *

AGREEMENT

Date:

Today, I searched through my home and removed the following pagan and superstitious objects:

_____

_____

Today, I also began to practice the custody of my senses, starting with:
- ☐ Custody of the Eyes
- ☐ Custody of the Ear
- ☐ Custody of the tongue
- ☐ Custody of Smell
- ☐ Custody of Tact
- ☐ All of them

Signature

_____

STEP FIVE

HOLY MASS AND EUCHARISTIC COMMUNION

P articipating in the perfect worship offered to the Lord during the Holy Mass is an important step on the path to holiness.

In the sacrifice of the Mass, we offer our highest form of worship and adoration to God. During Mass, God the Son offers Himself to God the Father through God the Holy Spirit, and nothing is more perfect than that.

It is essential to acknowledge that God does not need our worship or offerings, as He is perfect and self-sufficient. However, we offer Him worship as a matter of justice and gratitude, acknowledging His greatness and giving Him the honor and glory He deserves. Furthermore, worship is essential for humanity's existence.

Throughout the world, the Catholic Church celebrates a Eucharistic mass every second, This remarkable display of faith and devotion fulfills the prophecy in the scriptures:

"¹¹ For from the rising of the sun even to the going down, my name is great among the Gentiles, and in every place there is sacrifice, and there is offered to my name a clean oblation: for my name is great among the Gentiles, saith the Lord of hosts." **Malachi 1:11**

WHAT IS WORSHIP AND WHY DO WE WORSHIP GOD

Worship is like an umbilical cord of life that unites us to God. After the fall of our first parents, God instituted worship as a means of addressing the profound consequences of original sin. This grave offense severed the intimate and direct connection between humanity and God, leaving us without a vital source of life. As a result, it became necessary for humanity to find a way to reintegrate and re-establish this connection to continue existing.

God gave us the solution and taught Adam and Eve how to offer worship and sacrifice (Genesis 3:21). Through worship, we are able to fulfill this fundamental need and honor our relationship with God. Worship has been a continuous practice since the beginning of humanity, as we see in Genesis 4:4 and Gen 8:20-5.

WHY WAS ANIMAL SACRIFICE NECESSARY BEFORE THE TIME OF CHRIST?

When we commit sins, we incur a debt to God, and the payment is death, as stated in Romans 6:23. The question arises: how can we possibly repay this debt to the Almighty? Is it through material possessions or monetary offerings? The answer is no. The only thing we can offer that has any value is our life, our most precious asset. It is through our life that we can seek redemption. According to the Bible, life is in the blood; therefore, it is blood that we had to offer to God as a sacrifice to atone for our sins.

. . .

> *"11 Because the life of the flesh is in the blood: and I have given it to you, that you may make atonement with it upon the altar for your souls, and the blood may be for an expiation of the soul." (Leviticus 17:11)*

AS A RESULT OF SIN, our blood is tainted and cannot be presented to God as a sacrifice. Hence, a temporary solution was introduced to reconcile us with God after humanity fell from grace. This solution involved using the blood of animals for sacrifice since they were considered sinless. However, this temporary measure was not sufficient to atone for the original sin of disobedience committed against God in our perfect state before the fall. As a result, nobody could enter heaven before Jesus came. The Second Person of the Trinity took on human form and lived a sinless life among us. He then offered His blood as a sacrifice to atone for all our sins and reconcile us with God. Therefore, after Jesus' sacrifice, animal sacrifices were no longer needed.

To GIVE ourselves a better perspective we are going to exaggerate an example:

Picture a world where no human being worships or offers sacrifices to God. In such a world, Chaos would reign supreme, and destruction would be rampant. Everything would fall apart. This Godless state would make it impossible for humanity to survive, let alone thrive. Such a place already exists where nobody worships God, and it's called Hell.

God is the source of life, and our disconnection from God means we are disconnected from life itself. Worship is not just for our personal benefit but also for the betterment of humanity, including those who do not worship.

> One perfect act of worship in the world is enough to obtain God's grace for everyone and all of creation.

This is one of the reasons why the Church of Christ is called Catholic. The word Catholic comes from the Greek word 'katholikos,' which means 'universal.'

Remember: Attending Sunday's mass is mandatory, and failing to attend is a serious sin. We cannot worship God perfectly on our own because perfect worship requires a blood sacrifice, and Jesus' blood is the only one worthy to be presented before God. The Holy Mass offers Jesus' blood every day at every service. If we truly seek holiness, we should attend Mass as often as possible. Daily attendance is best, but at the very least, we should attend once a week in addition to fulfilling our Sunday obligations. When we attend Holy Mass, we receive the necessary graces for our salvation and collaborate with God's plan for salvation.

Let's read the Catechism of the Church 2181:

> "The Sunday Eucharist is the foundation and confirmation of all Christian practice. For this reason the faithful are **obliged to participate in the Eucharist on days of obligation**, unless excused for a serious reason (for example, illness, the care of infants) or dispensed by their own pastor.[119] **Those who deliberately fail in this obligation commit a grave sin**"[1]

MERCHANTS OR WORSHIPPERS?

The Church is the guardian and house of the tabernacle of the living God. It is a sacred place where we can experience his divine and physical presence. Every single deed performed within the Church's territory is magnified, and even the simplest task is enormously gratified. Something seemingly insignificant, such as picking up a piece of paper in the Church area, can bring us many blessings. Therefore, it is important to exercise mindfulness and show utmost respect for the house of the Lord. If we fail to do so, the exact opposite of what we expect may happen. Therefore, if we ever feel angry or frustrated, it is better to contain our emotions and step outside the perimeter of the Church. It'll be better for us.

To fully comprehend this, we must revisit the event where Jesus became angry in the temple. He witnessed the money changers conducting business within the confines of God's house. Despite the city of Jerusalem bustling with merchants, it was only within the temple precincts that Jesus' fury was sparked. His anger was amplified because the temple area is considered sacred. Let's read:

JOHN 2:13-17

> *"13 The Passover of the Jews was near, and Jesus went up to Jerusalem. 14 **In the temple** he found people selling cattle, sheep, and doves, and the money changers seated at their tables. 15 Making a whip of cords, he drove all of them **out of the temple**, both the sheep and the cattle. He also poured out the coins of the money changers and overturned their tables. 16 He told those who were selling the doves, "Take these things out of here! Stop making **my Father's house** a marketplace!" 17 His disciples remembered that it was written, "Zeal for your house will consume me."*

IN THE TEMPLE OF JERUSALEM, the sale of animals for sacrifice and the exchange of coins for offerings were carried out in an area called the Court of the Gentiles. Although this area was situated outside the Holy of Holies, it was still within the perimeter of the Temple. Jesus referred to this area as "my Father's house" and considered the offenses committed there as more serious. He wasn't concerned with the moneychanger's doing business outside the perimeter of the Temple.

Today, the temple of Jerusalem is represented by the sacred territory of the Church, with the Holy of Holies present in the Tabernacle. It should be treated with the utmost respect and veneration. It's important to remember that the entire area, not just the inside of the church, is sacred and deserves our reverence.

HOW CAN WE WORSHIP GOD PERFECTLY IF WE ARE IMPERFECT BEINGS?

Every human being owns God perfect adoration for themselves and the world.

It is important to understand that trying to replace the Holy Mass by praying at home is not enough. In our homes, we are unable to offer the body and blood of our Lord, which is essential to offer perfect worship. Without this vital element, we cannot attain that perfect adoration. The prayers we offer at home are valid, but they are not perfect.

> It is considered a serious sin for Catholics to miss Holy Mass because it means we are not cooperating with God's plan for salvation.

During mass, The Church, perfect in its divine nature, unites the three Churches of God—the militant Church (which is us), the suffering Church (which is the souls in purgatory), and the triumphant Church (which is those who are in Heaven). Each mass witnesses the presence of all three Churches, along with all the angels, Saints, Christ, Mary, the souls in purgatory, and us.

THE EUCHARIST IS NOT SYMBOLIC

In the Catholic mass, we honor God, and He is the focus of our worship. The purpose of the mass is not to entertain people. Some individuals may prefer attending other Christian services because they find them more "fun." However, they tend to forget that only in the Catholic Church do we have the real body and blood of Christ through the miracle of ***transubstantiation***. Our communion is not symbolic; it is true blood and true flesh that we receive through the power of apostolic succession, which is something that other Christian denominations lack. In contrast, their "communion" is just mere cookies and cheap wine that lack any true significance because they don't have the authority to transform a simple bread into the body of Christ.

> *john 6:53-56*
> *53 So Jesus said to them, "Very truly, I tell you, **unless you eat the flesh of the Son of Man and drink his blood**, you have no life in you. 54 Those who **eat my flesh and drink my blood** have eternal life, and I will raise them up on the last day; 55 for **my flesh is true food and my blood is true drink**.*

Satanic cults validate the apostolic Authority of the Catholic Church and the miracle of the Eucharist. Every year, they steal the blessed Eucharist to perform their black masses, especially on Halloween, which is their version of Christmas. They pay between $3,000 and $5,000 for a consecrated host taken only from a Catholic Church and use it in their rituals to desecrate it by urinating, spitting, defecating on it, and many other practices too gross to mention in this book. We wonder why they don't steal the bread and wine from other Christian denominations. It's impressive that these individuals cannot be fooled because they can differentiate between blessed and unblessed eucharistic bread. We are wondering why they go through the trouble of stealing the bread only from Catholics and paying a significant amount of money if it is just symbolic bread. Satanists won't pay a dime for the bread of a protestant denomination, and this is a fact.

lets read Matthew 26:26-28:

> **26** *While they were eating, Jesus took a loaf of bread, and after blessing it he broke it, gave it to the disciples, and said, "Take, eat;* **this is my body."** *27 Then he took a cup, and after giving thanks he gave it to them, saying, "Drink from it, all of you;* **28 for this is my blood** *of the[d] covenant, which is poured out for many for the forgiveness of sins.*

Note that Jesus did not say, "This is LIKE my body" or "This "represents" my blood." Jesus affirmed, "This IS MY BODY."

APOSTOLIC SUCCESSION

The Catholic Church, founded by Christ in the year 33 AD, has an unbroken chain of continuity dating back to the Apostles, as stated in Matthew 16:18:

> *18 And I say to thee: That thou art Peter; and upon this rock I will build* **my church***, and the gates of hell shall not prevail against it.*

Note that it doesn't say, "I will build my CHURCHES."

Nowadays, thousands of Protestant denominations continue to fracture and divide themselves, resulting in a vast array of churches and sects. They all claim to hold the truth, but they all disagree with each other. Nobody is on the same page, and even members of their congregation have their own interpretations of the scriptures. In contrast, the Catholic Church is the only one that has preserved the same teachings for over 2,000 years.

> *Ephesians 4:5*
> *"⁵ One Lord, **one** faith, one baptism."*

Here it says ONE FAITH, not "many" or "thousands."

It's important to understand that building a place of worship and creating your own regulations does not make a church identical to the Catholic Church just because they can copy what Catholics do. The problem with other Christian denominations is that they do not have Apostolic Succession.

In the Catholic Church, we can trace any priest's lineage back to Jesus and the apostles; this is impossible in Protestantism. No pastor can be traced back to the year 33.

Verbal Authority

Following his resurrection, Jesus appeared to his apostles and granted them the church's keys and the authority to make decisions regarding its administration. This authority, commonly referred to as the Power to Bind and Loose, empowers the Church of Christ to make doctrinal judgments, disciplinary decisions, and absolve sins through divine power.

We see this in Matthew 16:19:

> *⁹ I will give you the **keys** of the kingdom of heaven, and*

whatever you bind on earth will be bound in heaven, and whatever you loose on earth will be loosed in heaven.

SPIRITUAL AUTHORITY

After giving them the verbal authority, Jesus gave them spiritual authority through the power of the Holy Spirit:

> *john 20:22-23:*
> *²² When he had said this,* **he breathed on them** *and said to them, "Receive the Holy Spirit. ²³ If you* **forgive the sins** *of any,* **they are forgiven** *them; if you* **retain the sins** *of any,* **they are retained**.

This passage describes a powerful moment when Jesus imparts an extraordinary gift to his disciples: the power and authority to forgive sins. However, before granting them this incredible ability, he performs a special act: he breathes the Holy Spirit into them.

It's worth noting that the Holy Spirit is omnipresent, always existing everywhere. So why did Jesus choose to breathe it into his disciples? because it represented a unique and lasting gift that would continue to empower them long after he was gone.

In fact, this act is reminiscent of when God created Adam and breathed life into his nostrils, an eternal gift that passes from person to person. By breathing the Holy Spirit into his disciples, Jesus is symbolically granting them a new kind of life, one that is infused with divine power and authority.

> *Genesis 2:7:*
> *⁷ then the Lord God formed man from the dust of the*

ground,[a] and breathed into his nostrils the breath of life; and the man became a living being.

How did Adam pass on the gift of life to his children? He did not breathe on them because he was not the author of life. Life is transmitted through contact when sperm penetrates the egg. Similarly, Jesus breathed this power and authority onto his apostles, an eternal gift that passes from person to person. And how did the apostles pass on their power and authority to their successors? They did not breathe on them, as the Holy Spirit does not come from them, but rather it was given to them. Instead, they bestowed this power and authority through contact, specifically through the laying of hands.

The apostles, who were chosen by Jesus to spread his message, designated a successor before they died. This was done to ensure that the same power and authority Jesus gave them would be passed on to future generations. This power is the same power that forgives sins, transforms bread into the body and blood of Jesus during the transubstantiation, and inspired and collected the books of the Bible. No other denomination has a part in this apostolic succession. None.

PHYSICAL MOVEMENTS IN THE HOLY MASS

The Mass is a sacred encounter between God and humanity. We seek God's grace and blessings through heartfelt prayers, meaningful words, symbolic gestures, and movements. As human beings, we are a complex mixture of body, soul, and spirit, and

> we use our entire being to worship God during the Mass

Our physical movements during the Mass have deep spiritual significance and are not merely empty gestures. However,

Protestant denominations may not comprehend the significance of our bodily movements and may criticize them as worthless.

In the mass, we pour ourselves out to God in body and spirit. Nevertheless, every movement during the Mass has a specific purpose, and we perform them with complete devotion and commitment to God.

> *Romans 12*
> *"I BESEECH you therefore, brethren, by the mercy of God, that you **present your bodies a living sacrifice, holy, pleasing unto God**, your reasonable service."*

WHEN WE STAND, we show our respect for the moment and the people involved. It is a gesture of honor, a way to acknowledge the importance of the situation. On the other hand, when we kneel, we do it humbly to an almighty God, recognizing our smallness compared to his divinity. It shows our reverence and submission. Finally, when we sit down, we assume a receptive posture, ready to listen and learn from the message we are about to receive. We open our minds and hearts to the word of God.

As Catholics, our relationship with God is not only spiritual but also physical. We unite with Him by consuming His flesh and blood, becoming one with Him. Through this sacrament, we can taste, see, and touch Jesus.

HUMAN TABERNACLES

It is important to understand that receiving the sacred host is both a privilege and a responsibility. When we consume the body and blood of Christ, we become living tabernacles. This is like when a priest places the consecrated host in the monstrance for Eucharistic adoration. Essentially, we become the monstrance ourselves.

The digestion process in our body can take anywhere from 40 minutes to 2 hours, depending on the complexity of the food we consume. However, the digestion time may be shorter for simpler meals, ranging from 30 to 60 minutes. In contrast, water is absorbed much faster, with a typical absorption time of 10 to 20 minutes. This information is particularly relevant when we consider the Eucharist because after receiving it, we become a living tabernacle that hosts the body of Christ for approximately 30 minutes to an hour. During this time, the sacred bread is gradually absorbed and integrated into our bodies.

EUCHARISTIC INSTRUMENTS OF REPARATION

When we receive communion in a state of grace, we become Eucharistic instruments of reparation, and the Lord rescues souls. After attending mass, we carry Christ's real presence within us, radiating His love and grace to those around us. Whether we stop at the grocery store or drive home, God blesses the people who come into our path, bringing about miraculous events that we may not even be aware of. Accidents are prevented, people are healed, life is preserved, and souls are transformed.

This reminds us of the biblical account of Peter, whose very shadow brought healing to the sick and broken as he walked. Through the power of the Eucharist, Peter became a living tabernacle, a vessel of God's healing love overflowing to all those around him. (Acts 5:15)

How often do we find ourselves arguing with our spouse or children or cursing at people blocking traffic as we leave mass? How often do we use profanity and make mean comments, gossip, or get drunk without realizing that the Lord is still present in our bodies even after mass?

The Eucharistic presence extends over a vast geographical location, encompassing an area whose actual size remains unknown. The graces bestowed upon us do not end when we leave the church; our entire neighborhood and perhaps even the whole town can benefit from them. This is because all Catholics who take communion and leave the church become walking tabernacles, carrying within them the living God.

THE MIRACLE OF THE INCORRUPT BODIES

The Eucharist is a source of spiritual nourishment that helps us avoid situations of mortal sin and awakens the gifts of the Holy Spirit within us. Consuming the Eucharist transforms us into Christ-like people, like a spiritual blood transfusion. We can see evidence of this transformation in the incorrupt bodies of the Saints, a miracle that occurs only through the Eucharist.

This miracle is God's divine gift to his church; no other religious group ever had or will have such a miracle. We will never see a Protestant Pastor with an incorrupt body, nor a Jew or a Muslim, no matter how holy they may be. This miracle only happens in our Catholic Church through the power of the Eucharist.

All these wonders can happen if we are obedient to God. However, consuming the Eucharist while in a state of mortal sin can put us at risk of diabolical possession or expose us to situations that lead us to commit more mortal sins. To ensure that the Eucharist has the proper effect on us, we must practice obedience to God and frequently go to confession to keep ourselves in a state of grace.

EUCHARISTIC MIRACLES

Throughout history, there have been numerous accounts of Eucharistic Miracles worldwide in which the sacred host has undergone a physical transformation into flesh and blood. One of the most popular is the eucharistic miracle of Lanciano, Italy. These miraculous events have been the subject of extensive study and analysis by numerous scientists and medical professionals from different backgrounds.

Using advanced science, researchers have examined the physical changes that occur during these Eucharistic Miracles, examining the properties of the transformed host. Medical professionals have also analyzed the blood samples from miraculous events, studying the DNA and blood type to determine whether they are human in origin, returning fantastic results. One commonality is that the flesh discovered originates from human heart muscle. Furthermore, the tissue contains white blood cells, which is a clear indication that the tissue is still alive. The blood found is also of type AB, known as a universal receiver. However, what is particularly intriguing is that the blood only has one chromosome X, which suggests that the DNA is incomplete. Although the chromosomes for the mother can be identified, none can be found for the father. These Eucharistic Miracles serve as a testament to the miraculous workings of God in our world.

Message of the Virgin in Medjugorje:

> **April 25, 1988** "Dear children! God wants to make you holy. Therefore, through me He is inviting you to complete surrender. Let holy mass be your life. Understand that the church is God's palace, the place in which I gather you and want to show you the way to God. Come and pray. Neither look at others nor slander them, but rather, let your life be

a testimony on the way of holiness. Churches deserve respect and are set apart as holy because God, who became man, dwells in them day and night. Therefore, little children, believe and pray that the Father increase your faith, and then ask for whatever you need. I am with you and I am rejoicing because of you conversion and I am protecting you with my motherly mantle. Thank you for having responded to my call."[2]

FREQUENCY:

We must attend Holy Mass and receive communion as often as possible, in addition to our Sunday obligation.

* * *

AGREEMENT

Date:

Today, I attended a weekday mass, and today, I pledge to attend mass _____ times a week in addition to my Sunday obligation.

Signature:

_____

11

STEP SIX

EUCHARISTIC ADORATION OF THE BLESSED SACRAMENT

Adoration is a profoundly intimate encounter with Jesus in the exposed blessed sacrament. As we approach Him with humility and reverence, we enter a sacred and holy space where Jesus conceals His humanity in the eucharist, just as He once concealed His divinity on the cross. We are enveloped in His radiant glory, and He communicates His grace to us in a unique and direct way. This is a place of profound spiritual connection, an antechamber to Heaven where we are granted a glimpse of the divine. It is like being transported into the Holy of Holies, the innermost sanctuary of the Temple in Jerusalem, where only the High Priest was allowed to enter once a year.

Let's read Hebrews 9:7

> "But into the second, the high priest alone, once a year:
> not without blood, which he offereth for his own,
> and the people's ignorance:"

As we step into this sacred place, we must approach it with utmost reverence. We bow our heads and prostrate ourselves because we are standing in the presence of the King of the universe. Once we enter the chamber of adoration, we are immediately enveloped by God's divine glory. This experience stays with us long after we leave this holy sanctuary, and its profound impact spreads blessings and graces to those around us.

Moses' face shone after being in God's presence, and the Jews were afraid, so they covered his face with a veil (Exodus 34:29).

It reminds us of the glow we experience in God's presence, a spiritual brightness that is imperceptible to the naked eye. This practice is an essential element of our path to righteousness.

Saint Carlos Acutis said:

> "When we face the sun we get a tan…but when we stand before Jesus in the Eucharist **we become saints.**"[1]

Saint Alphonsus Maria de Liguori:

> "Know that you will perhaps gain more **in a quarter of an hour of adoration** in the presence of the Blessed Jesus than in all the other spiritual exercises of the day."

Saint Teresa of Calcutta:

> "The time one spends with Jesus in the Blessed Sacrament is the time best spent on Earth,"

As we settle into our chosen spot, we continue in contemplation and prayer. Some of us recite the rosary, novenas, litanies, or other devotions, while others sit and talk to the Lord as if He were their best friend or a dear Father. Some share their joys and blessings, while others pour out their hearts and souls, unburdening themselves of their worries and fears. We stay as long as we need to, some for just a few minutes, others for hours, and some even stay all night, taking turns accompanying the Lord.

All the Saints practiced adoration to the Blessed Sacrament.

As we prepare to leave this sacred space, it is important to consider the significance of our exit. Many people demonstrate reverence and admiration by prostrating or kneeling as a sign of adoration and farewell. This act of humility and respect acknowledges the divine presence that surrounds us and honors the sanctity of the space we are leaving. Others prefer to take a different approach. Rather than turn their backs to the blessed sacrament, they walk backward until they exit the room. This gesture demonstrates a deep reverence and humility, allowing us to connect with the divine presence even as we leave the physical space. Regardless of which approach we choose, it is essential to remember that we are in the presence of the Creator. As such, our exit should be filled with the utmost respect and veneration, recognizing the sacredness of the space we are leaving and the divine presence that permeates it.

THE VIRGIN IN Medjugorje tells us:

> "Let the Most Holy Sacrament of the Altar be Adored without interruption. I am always present when the faithful are in Adoration. At that moment, **particular graces are obtained.**"[2]

How often do we practice adoration of the Most Holy Sacrament?

We should aim to participate in this practice at least once a week. However, it's important to note that doing it less or more often doesn't necessarily mean we're doing it wrong. If we've chosen to walk the path of holiness, like the Saints, we should make Eucharistic adoration a regular part of our routine and strive to go above and beyond the minimum requirement.

> "There is no Saint who is not an adorer of the Holy One."

* * *

AGREEMENT

Date:

Today, I went to Eucharistic adoration, and I pledge to practice this devotion every
 ☐ week
 ☐ month.

Signature:

_____

12

STEP SEVEN

THE HOLY ROSARY

The Holy Rosary is one of the most powerful tools in the Church. It is a powerful spiritual protection, acting like a sturdy fence that encircles and shields us from the forces of evil. The doors of this fence are represented by the Our Father, and the fence that surrounds us is represented by each Hail Mary. The rosary helps us stay in a state of grace. It is a shortcut to Heaven. However, we must be mindful that a poorly made prayer in the rosary is like a poorly placed fence, which allows the evil one to enter. Thus, it is crucial to approach the rosary with the utmost reverence and care to benefit from its spiritual protection.

THE ROSARY, A FISHING NET

The rosary is a spiritual tool that can be likened to a fishing net thrown into the sea to catch fish. Similarly, through the power of the rosary, we can catch and help our relatives and brothers from all around the world, no matter how far apart we may be physically. The rosary is a powerful instrument enabling us to help humanity from a distance and potentially touch and transform countless lives.

Many of us feel a deep sense of helplessness when we think about the suffering of those in distant lands, for example, the hungry children in Africa. Although we may be able to help a few, it is impossible to help everyone. However, the rosary can penetrate all corners of the world and help those in need. We can fight against hunger, wars, diseases, and many other social ills through the power of the rosary. Through the rosary, we can intercede for the redemption of those who have committed sins like adultery, abortion, murder, etc. As members of the militant Church, it is our duty to intercede for the world and to use the rosary to steal souls from Satan.

When we start praying the rosary for the first time, we may face intimidation from the evil one. He may even target our loved ones or pets if he can't harm us directly. Therefore, if we experience such attacks, we should not be discouraged and continue with our prayers.

The rosary is a powerful sacramental that has been used for centuries as a tool for prayer and protection. It's always advisable to keep a rosary close by for easy access, such as in the car, purse, bedside, or even worn around the neck.

PRAYING THE ROSARY IN LATIN

The rosary was originally prayed and taught in Latin, a sacred language that creates a sacred veil over our prayers. Many exorcists recommend praying in Latin. The Vatican's chief exorcist, Father Gabriele Amorth, who performed more than 70,000 exorcisms, testified to the power conferred on this sacred language:

> "It's more effective in defying the devil."

. . .

BISHOP ANDREA GEMMA OF ISERNIA, one of the Roman Catholic Church's leading experts on exorcism, explained:

> "Demons have a horror of the [Latin] language." He later stated, "The devil is content with the near disappearance of Latin."[1]

Latin was one of the languages that was inscribed on the Cross. **INRI** means: **Iesus Nazarenus Rex Iudaeorum** (Jesus of Nazareth, King of the Jews)

Latin was a consecrated language of the Church due to its use for more than 2,000 years (Pope John XXIII, Veterum Sapientia, 1962). Ecumenical councils have prescribed prayer in Latin. The royal texts of Vatican II mandated the retention of Latin in the liturgy:

> "... The use of the Latin language is to be preserved in the Latin rites" (36). "However, measures must be taken to ensure that the faithful may also say or sing together in Latin those parts of the Ordinary of the Mass which correspond to them" (54).[2]

Many saints have used Latin in their prayers. Latin is a pure language and is not associated with profanity or pornography.

> "[Latin is] the language of the angels." (Pope Paul VI, *General Audience, Nov 26, 1969*).

SLOW AND MEDITATED

To pray the Rosary properly, take your time and reflect on each mystery while being mindful of every word spoken. We are often criticized for praying the rosary because it is repetitive. However, the rosary is like the heartbeat of our prayers. Just as the heart beats to pump life into the body, the repetitive prayers of the rosary are the heartbeats that keep our prayers alive. Similarly, breathing is repetitive and necessary for life. Therefore, the rosary is a spiritual organ that helps us keep our prayers alive, however, It is easy to fall into the habit of rushing through the prayer, repeating the words automatically and without thought. This way of praying eliminates piety.

St. Louis Marie de Montfort tells us:

> "It is not so much the length of a prayer, but the fervor with which it is said that pleases Almighty God and touches His Heart. A single Hail Mary well said is worth more than a hundred and fifty badly spoken."

St. Josemaría Escrivá says:

> "The Rosary is not prayed only with the lips, murmuring Hail Marys one after the other. That's how overly pious old men and women recite them in one sitting. "For the Christian, vocal prayer must spring from the heart, so that while praying the Rosary, the mind may enter into the contemplation of each of the mysteries." (Furrow, No. 477)

In the apparitions of Garabandal, Our Lady taught the visionaries to pray the Holy Rosary; the mystics tell us:

> "We need to think about what we're praying for. To pray is to speak with God and with Our Lady. When we say the Lord's Prayer or the Hail Mary, we are talking to God and the Virgin Mary, and we

should say them as when we speak to a person we love very much, **slowly and from the heart**."

BETTER TO PRAY THAN NOT TO PRAY

Many of us lead busy and hectic lives, and finding time to pray can be challenging. However, we often make the mistake of delaying it for later and end up not praying it at all. Sometimes, we are too consumed by our daily routine; at other times, we might feel too lazy to pray. But we must remember that we can always find time to pray the rosary, even if we can't pray it entirely. It's better to pray it incompletely than not pray it at all.

The rosary is a powerful prayer that strengthens our faith, calms our minds, and brings us closer to God.

St. Joseph Mary Escriva tells us in this regard:

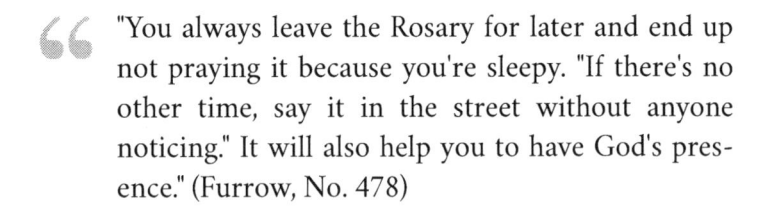

> "You always leave the Rosary for later and end up not praying it because you're sleepy. "If there's no other time, say it in the street without anyone noticing." It will also help you to have God's presence." (Furrow, No. 478)

PRAYING WITH REVERENCE

The apparitions of Our Lady have provided us with a unique way of praying that demands utmost respect when addressing the Holy Trinity. Over time, we have understood that this way of praying requires reverence and deep devotion. To illustrate this, we can look at how the Angel of the Apparitions of Fatima taught the little shepherds:

> " He knelt, **bending his forehead to the ground**. With a supernatural impulse we did the same, repeating the words we heard him say:

My God, I believe, I adore, I hope, and I love You. I ask pardon for those who do not believe, do not adore, do not hope, and do not love You.

After repeating this prayer three times the angel rose and said to us:

Pray in this way. The hearts of Jesus and Mary are ready to listen to you.

And he disappeared."[3]

During his address to the Holy Trinity, the Angel prostrated himself with his forehead on the ground and repeated the prayers we say in the rosary. Before leaving, he instructed to *"pray like this.."*

In the third apparition, the Angel prostrated himself again on the ground as he said the prayer we use today at the beginning of our rosary.:

> " While we were there, the angel appeared to us for the third time, holding in his hand a chalice, and above the chalice, a Host, from which a few drops of blood were falling. Leaving the chalice and Host suspended in air, **he prostrated himself on the ground** and repeated three times this prayer:
>
> "Most Holy Trinity, Father, Son and Holy Spirit, I adore You profoundly, and I offer You the most precious body, blood, soul and divinity of Jesus Christ, present in all the tabernacles of the world, in reparation for the outrages, sacrileges and indifference by which He is offended. And by the infinite merits of His most Sacred Heart and through the Immaculate Heart of Mary, I beg the conversion of poor sinners."[4]
>
> Afterward, he rose and took again the chalice and the Host and gave the Host to me and the

contents of the chalice to Jacinta and Francisco, saying to them:

"Take and drink the body and blood of Jesus Christ, horribly outraged by ungrateful men. Repair their crimes and console your God."[5]

Once more, **he prostrated himself and repeated with us three times the prayer**, "Most Holy Trinity... etc." He then disappeared."[6]

The Virgin bowed her head at each Gloria with extraordinary reverence in the apparitions of Garabandal and other apparitions.

THE GENERAL INSTRUCTION of the Roman Missal says in no. 275:

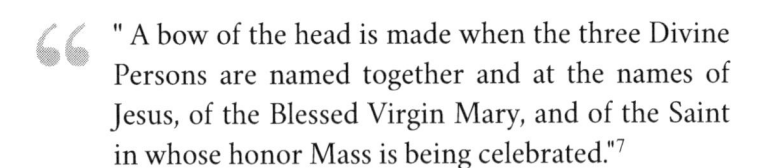

> " A bow of the head is made when the three Divine Persons are named together and at the names of Jesus, of the Blessed Virgin Mary, and of the Saint in whose honor Mass is being celebrated."[7]

Bowing down to every Glory or Our Father conveys a message of high reverence for them. In light of this, we might wonder how best to incorporate this practice into our recitation of the Holy Rosary. Learning from the insights gained through the apparitions of Our Lady, how might we modify our approach to this cherished prayer? Bowing the head or prostrating when reciting:

> Most Holy Trinity, Father, Son, and Holy Spirit, I adore you deeply...
> Our Father who art in Heaven...

> Glory be to the Father, and to the Son, and to the Holy Spirit...
>
> My God, I believe, I adore, I hope, and I love you...

In the Book of Spiritual Exercises, number 76, St. Ignatius writes:

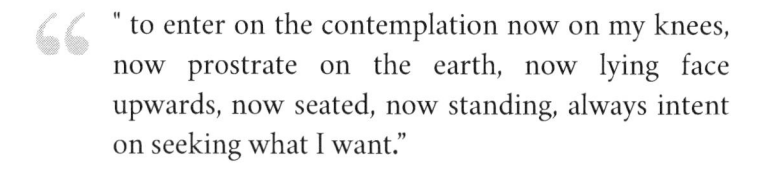

> " to enter on the contemplation now on my knees, now prostrate on the earth, now lying face upwards, now seated, now standing, always intent on seeking what I want."

> " The need to involve the senses in interior prayer corresponds to a requirement of our human nature. We are body and spirit, and we experience the need to translate our feelings externally. We must pray with **our whole being** to give all power possible to our supplication." *Catechism 2702.*[8]
>
> "God seeks worshippers in Spirit and in Truth, and consequently living prayer that rises from the depths of the soul. **He also wants the external expression that associates the body with interior prayer, for it renders Him that perfect homage which is His due**" (CCC 2703).[9]

IN THE BIBLE, we find this kind of worship:

- Abraham prostrates himself before the angels (Gen 18:2)

- His grandson Lot does the same "face to the ground" (Gen 19:1)
- Abraham's servant bowed down to the ground before the Lord (Gen 24:52)
- Jacob fell to the ground seven times (Gen 33:3)
- The brothers bow down before Joseph (Gen 42:6)

Many orthodox monks and priests still practice this prayer posture. prostration is also used in the consecration of a priest.

> **Prostration** is the quintessential expression of adoration as a gesture of humility.

The Rosary is our greatest ally. Our Lady, in her apparitions, calls us to pray the rosary every day. In the second apparition of Fatima, Our Lady said to Lucia:

> "I want you to pray the Rosary **every day.**"

Our Lady to the visionary Jacob in the apparitions of Medjugorje:

> "Dear children, may all the prayers you make tonight be for the conversion of sinners because the world is in grave sin. **Pray the Rosary every night.**"

Padre Pio prayed approximately 36 rosaries daily, and all the saints also prayed the rosary daily. The rosary and Mary's intercession are important allies on the path to holiness.

FREQUENCY:
We must pray the Rosary every day

THE PATH TO HOLINESS

* * *

AGREEMENT

Date:

Today, I began reciting the Holy Rosary, and I pledge to continue praying it every.

☐ Day
  ☐ Week
  ☐ Month

Signature:

13

STEP EIGHT

INTERCESSORY PRAYER

Intercessory prayer is the fundamental duty of every Catholic. As members of the universal Church, we are called to pray for everyone, including those unrelated to us, that is, all of humanity. Catholics have access to all the tools for salvation, and these tools are not exclusive to Catholics. We are meant to share these tools with our brothers and sisters around the world, as this is how we collaborate with God's plan of salvation and help the world from our homes.

INSTRUMENTS OF SALVATION

Catholics are chosen from our mother's womb as instruments of God's salvific plan for the world; similar to how the Jews were chosen to prepare the world for the arrival of the Messiah. Catholics are also considered to have a significant role in carrying out God's plan for the redemption of humanity. As such, we are expected to live in a way that reflects our faith and share the Church's teachings with others.

Jeremiah 1:5
"Before I formed you in the womb I knew you,
and before you were born I consecrated you;
I appointed you a prophet to the nations."

CATHOLICS ARE responsible for the salvation of all souls because God gave us the necessary knowledge and tools for this purpose.

LET's read John 17:6:11

"I have made your name known to those whom you gave me from the world. They were yours, and you gave them to me, and they **have kept your word***. ⁷ Now they know that everything you have given me is from you; ⁸ for the words that you gave to me I have given to them, and* **they have received them** *and know in truth that I came from you; and they have believed that you sent me."*

Who accepted Jesus' message? Christians who called themselves Catholics (Universal), and to this day, we maintain the integrity of the true Church of Jesus Christ.

From the beginning of Christianity, our prayers, devotions, and traditions have been geared toward serving humanity. We do not solely pray for ourselves, saying, "Oh my Jesus, forgive MY sins," "St. Michael the archangel, defend ME in battle," or "Pray for ME and MY FRIENDS, oh Holy Mother of God." Rather, we come together as a community to pray for the betterment of the world, and to be used by God as instruments of salvation. For instance, every time we attend Mass and partake in the Eucharist, the Lord rescues souls.

As part of the mystical body of Christ, every time we pray,

we can help the world from our homes with intercessory prayers. When we offer our fasting, mortification, and suffering and keep ourselves in a state of grace, we collaborate with God's plan.

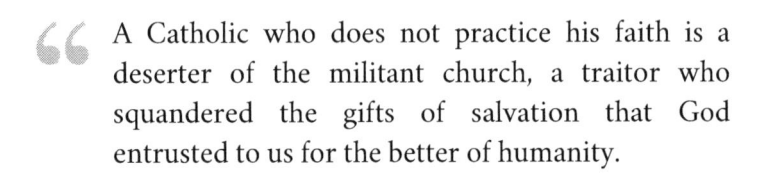

> A Catholic who does not practice his faith is a deserter of the militant church, a traitor who squandered the gifts of salvation that God entrusted to us for the better of humanity.

A LUKEWARM CATHOLIC will fall into a state of spiritual malnutrition and will be held accountable for the misuse of those gifts, the souls that could have been saved through him, and the graces he wasted.

SAINT CYPRIAN TEACHES:

> "When we pray, we are not to pray for ourselves alone. We do not say, "My Father, who art in heaven," or "Give me this day, my daily bread." We do not ask for our own trespasses alone to be forgiven, and when we pray that we may be delivered from evil, we are not only praying for ourselves. Our prayer is for the general good, for the common good. When we pray, we do not pray for our own single selves; **we pray for all God's people, because they and we are one.**"[1]

Frequency:
Everyday

* * *

AGREEMENT

Date:

Today, I began praying for people foreign to my flesh and blood. I commit to praying for those who suffer whenever I see a misfortune on the news or social media.

Signature:

_____

14

STEP NINE

THE COMMANDMENTS

Now that our house (soul) is clean and protected, the next step is decorating it. Let's start by conquering the Ten Commandments. As we know, the commandments have both literal and spiritual meaning.

For example, many people think that the fifth commandment, "*You shall not kill*," is the easiest to follow because most people do not physically harm anyone. However, the spiritual meaning of not killing also includes not slandering or speaking ill of our neighbor because our words can hurt them. The goal is to try and follow all the commandments to the best of our ability. To start, we can choose one commandment, for example, "*You shall not steal*," and practice it until we master it. We can then move on to the other commandments, doing the same until we improve on each one. We will make mistakes, but living in holiness requires persevering in the fight. Practicing the commandments begins at home with our family. What does Jesus tell us about the Ten Commandments?

> "*If you wish to enter into life, keep the commandments*"
> (Matthew 19:17)

. . .

THE COMMANDMENTS ARE WRITTEN in the heart of every human being.

> *Romans 2:14-16*
> " *When Gentiles, who do not possess the law, do **instinctively** what the law requires, these, though not having the law, are a law to themselves. [15] They show that what the law requires **is written on their hearts**, to which their own conscience also bears witness; and their conflicting thoughts will accuse or perhaps excuse them [16] on the day when, according to my gospel, God, through Jesus Christ, **will judge the secret thoughts of all..**"*

> *Hebrews 8:10*
> " *or this is the testament which I will make to the house of Israel after those days, saith the Lord: I will give my laws into their mind, **and in their heart will I write them**: and I will be their God, and they shall be my people."*

FREQUENCY: Everyday

* * *

AGREEMENT

Date:

Today, I will begin to master the following commandment:

_____

And I commit to working on conquering the remaining ones.

Signature:

_____

15

STEP TEN

BIBLE READING

Daily Bible reading is essential for individuals seeking to achieve a state of holiness. Every word within the Holy Bible produces a profound spiritual effect on us, even if we cannot perceive it. Whenever we read the Bible, we effectively recite the very words of God, which were divinely inspired and carry immense graces. Through this practice, we nourish our souls with the word of God.

> Matthew 4:4
> " It is written, Not in bread alone doth man live, but in **every word that proceedeth from the mouth of God..'"**

Bible readings are like seeds of life planted in our souls through the Holy Spirit. These seeds will bear fruit according to our spiritual state. God's word has a purpose and an effect; nothing we read is wasted.

Isaiah 55:11:
" so shall my word be that goes out from my mouth;
it shall not return to me empty,
but it shall accomplish that which I purpose,
and succeed in the thing for which I sent it.."

THE WORD of God is alive and is the source of divine revelation. In the word, we find the Holy Trinity. The word comes from God the Father, who is the first person of the Trinity, and he has revealed himself through his word. The word of God is embodied in God the Son, Jesus Christ, who through all things were created (Colossians 1:16-17). Additionally, The Holy Spirit is the one who manifests the word of God to all humanity. (John 1)

God is the God of the living. His creations are not finite or mortal but eternal. The Word of God is also full of life and always returns to its source. At the beginning of time, God created Adan with his breath and spoke the world into existence and everything in creation; therefore, plants and animals also have an everlasting soul because the word of God is eternal and never dies. Each creature has a specific purpose on this earth, and after fulfilling its purpose, it will return to its Creator. Only us humans must decide if we want to spend eternity with God.

ARE ALL BIBLES THE SAME?

As Catholics, we should be cautious when selecting a Bible. Many versions of the Bible have been modified to fit the pagan agenda of sects. The Bible contains 73 books, and it has been that way since the first official compilation made by the guardian of the holy doctrine, our Catholic Church. Any Bible with fewer than 73 books is incomplete. Catholics should not use those Bibles except for study, research, or as part of our apologetic material for teaching, refuting, or correcting purposes. (2 Timothy 3:16)

WHERE DO I START READING?

The Holy Bible can be approached in various ways. One can read a specific book, such as Genesis, Acts, or Wisdom, or select verses, paragraphs, or texts. However, the most effective and rewarding approach is to read the entire Bible from cover to cover, examining each letter with care and reverence. Though this may take a few years, it is a powerful way to deepen our spiritual journey and gain a profound understanding of God's voice, style, and personality. Additionally, we will be better equipped to discern false or misleading interpretations of the Scriptures.

UNDERSTANDING THE HOLY SCRIPTURES

The Catholic Church deeply respects the interpretation of the scriptures, believing that it should not be taken lightly or done according to individual preferences or convenience. Instead, the scriptures have been interpreted and handed down to us by the apostles, the Fathers of the Church, and the Magisterium of the Church. This unbroken chain of teachings has been passed down for over two millennia, beginning with the apostles.

On the other hand, Protestant denominations do not have a unified Church structure, and each denomination, Pastor, and member have their own interpretation of the Holy Scriptures. This leads to a proliferation of new denominations and a fragmentation of beliefs, resulting in a never-ending cycle of new Protestant denominations. This is in stark contrast to the early Christian teaching, which relies on the unity of the Church to provide a consistent and unchanging interpretation of the scriptures for all believers.

It is of utmost importance to steer clear of any confusion that may arise and strictly adhere to the teachings of the Catholic Church. In case of any uncertainties, consulting only authentic Catholic sources is highly recommended. Why seek answers from Protestant sources with an incomplete Bible consisting of only 66 books? Why go to an incomplete source when we have the fullness of the truth in the Catholic Church? Relying on their incomplete material could lead to erroneous interpretations. Instead, we should repose our trust in the Catholic Church, which has held and transmitted the same message of truth for over two millennia.

> *John 10:27:*
> *"My sheep hear my voice, and I know them, and they follow me."*

READING FROM THE HEART

Before embarking on our scriptural readings, it is essential that we pray to the Holy Spirit to grant us the gift of comprehension and insight into God's wonderful word. St. Ephraim the Syrian advises us:

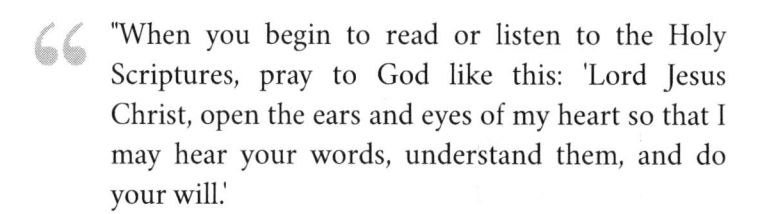

> "When you begin to read or listen to the Holy Scriptures, pray to God like this: 'Lord Jesus Christ, open the ears and eyes of my heart so that I may hear your words, understand them, and do your will.'

The Holy Bible is a sacred text that demands our utmost respect and devotion. When we approach it for reading, we kiss it before and after each reading, a customary sign of reverence. To truly benefit from the wisdom within its pages, we must read the scriptures attentively, meditating on each passage and reflecting on its message.

May our minds understand the word of God. may our mouths proclaim the truth, and may our hearts be filled with the fulness of his word

Jesus asked St. Faustina to read the Bible slowly and thoughtfully:

> "During his retreat on June 2, 1938... Jesus commanded St. Faustina to read the Bible (see St. Faustina's Diary, 1751). In #1757, He said to her, "Today you will read the fifteenth chapter of the Gospel of St. John. **I want you to read it slowly.**" In the 1765 Diary entry, He said to her, "Today, My child, by your reading, You will take the nineteenth chapter of the Gospel of St. John and read it, not only with your lips, **but with your heart.**"

To truly understand and embrace the message of God, we must approach the Bible with an open heart and mind, even if, at times, the message may challenge or go against our personal beliefs and preferences.

God's message has remained consistent throughout time. As a Holy text, the Bible cannot be molded to our personal preferences and lifestyles. There isn't such a thing as an "old-fashioned" Bible. The Bible is always in fashion. Instead, it calls us to align our lives with the divine truth and wisdom contained within its pages. In essence, we must strive to adapt ourselves to the will of God rather than expecting Him to cater to our sinful needs and desires.

What does St. Augustine tell us about this?

> "If you believe in the gospels what you like and reject what you don't like, you don't believe in the gospel, but in yourself."

ADDITIONAL SUPPORTING MATERIALS

To gain a deeper understanding, it is highly recommended that we supplement our reading of the Bible with other Catholic sources. These books can provide valuable insights into the teachings of revered figures such as Saints, Theologians, and the Fathers of the Church and explore important doctrines. St. John Bosco tells us:

> "Only God knows the good that can result from reading a good Catholic book."

St. Padre Pio advises:

> "Help yourself during this turbulent period by reading holy books. This reading provides excellent nourishment for the soul and leads to great progress on the path of perfection. It is in no way inferior to what we gain through prayer and holy meditation. In prayer and meditation it is we ourselves who speak to the Lord, while in holy reading it is God who speaks to us. Before you begin to read, lift up your mind to the Lord and implore Him Himself to guide your mind, to speak to your heart, and to move your will."

If you are a Catholic and looking for a devotional book to help you learn how to imitate Jesus, then "Imitation of Christ" is a must-read for you. This book is considered a religious classic and has been widely read since its publication. It was printed 745 times before 1650 and translated into more languages than any other book after the Bible. The popularity of "Imitation of Christ" can be attributed to its simple yet powerful message. It has been called "the most influential work of Christian literature" and "the fifth gospel." The "Imitation of Christ" can help us understand the essence of Christian life and provide guidance on how to live a virtuous life. It is a timeless work that can inspire us to become a better person and deepen our faith. So, to learn how to follow in Jesus' footsteps, consider adding "Imitation of Christ" to your reading list.

USEFUL USES

The Bible is a holy book that contains the sacred word of God and deserves the utmost respect. It is not merely a decorative item to be used as a cup holder or a lucky charm. The only acceptable items to place on top of a Bible are another Bible or perhaps a rosary. We often encounter an immaculate, unopened Bible when visiting someone's house. We can see that no one has read or studied it. The Bible must be used. If we don't use it, what do we have it for? So, let us dust off our Bibles and dive into the pages.

A helpful practice is to inscribe bible verses in various places around our home. Whether on the walls, windows, furniture or even on the bed frame, it helps us memorize and internalize scripture, which can be helpful in moments of need. Moreover, these verses can shield against negative influences, making the home a peaceful and sacred place. This will remind us of God's word, help us learn scriptures, and protect the house.

Words of the Virgin in her appearances in Medjugorje:

> "Dear children! Today I invite you to read the Bible every day in your homes; place it in a conspicuous place, so that it may always encourage you to read it and to pray..."

> "Dear children! I reveal to you a spiritual secret: if you want to be stronger against evil, become an active conscience. For this, pray a lot in the morning and read a text from the Gospel. Engrave the divine Word in your hearts and live it during the day, especially in trials, and at night you will be stronger."

FREQUENCY
Read the bible every day

* * *

AGREEMENT

Date:

Today I will begin reading the Holy Bible and commit to reading it every:
  ☐ Day
  ☐ Week
  ☐ Month

Signature:

_____

16

STEP ELEVEN

PIOUS PRACTICES AND DEVOTIONS

Practices of piety refer to the various ways we can reach out to God through the Church Triumphant. These practices include calling out for help, offering praise, honoring God, and participating in his plan for salvation. The list of pious practices is extensive and covers a wide range of devotions, including devotions to the Saints, reciting litanies, participating in the stations of the cross, making consecrations to the Virgin, showing devotion to St. Michael and our guardian angel, and going on pilgrimages. These practices are ways to deepen our faith and connect with God in a meaningful way.

LET'S TALK ABOUT SOME OF THESE DEVOTIONAL PRACTICES.

Litanies

Litanies are an ancient form of prayer that involves reciting or singing a series of invocations. These invocations are typically directed towards God, the Virgin Mary, or various Saints. One of the most beautiful litanies is the litany of humility, which is unique in that it challenges our natural inclination to prioritize our needs and desires over those of others. Doing so helps us overcome one of the deadliest enemies, pride, and encourages us to develop a humbler and more selfless mindset.

Another popular devotion is the 15 prayers of St. Bridget. They are prayers of adoration and contemplation of the passion of Jesus. St. Bridget wanted to know how many lashes Our Lord had received in His Passion. One day Jesus Christ appeared to her saying:

> "I received 5475 blows to my body. If you wish to honor them in any way, recite 15 Our Fathers and 15 Hail Marys with the following prayers for a full year, which I Myself will teach you. By the end of the year, you will have honored every one of my wounds."

This prayer demands dedication and commitment, requiring daily practice for an entire year. Only those brave enough to embark on this journey can undertake it. However, according to reports, the blessings are abundant. This prayer is accompanied by 15 promises that Jesus revealed to St. Bridget, which adds a sense of profound significance and meaning to the practice.

Marian Consecrations

Am I not here, who am your Mother?' -Virgen of Guadalupe to San Diego

Mary is not only the mother of Jesus but also the mother of all humanity. As such, she is highly revered and respected by Catholics worldwide. One way in which we express our devotion to Mary is by participating in various religious practices and rituals. These include reciting the Rosary, wearing scapulars, praying litanies, reciting the Angelus, practicing devotion to the Immaculate Heart of Mary, participating in the devotion of the five first Saturdays, wearing the miraculous medal, and meditating on the seven sorrows of the Virgin. These devotions serve as a way for us to connect with our Mother and seek her intercession on our behalf, as we believe she is the Queen of Heaven.

Marian's consecration is a powerful way to deepen this devotion. It involves entrusting oneself entirely to Our Lady's protection, guidance, and intercession. This act of consecration is a formal recognition of Mary's role as one's spiritual mother and Queen. Traditionally, Marian consecrations involve a period of thirty-three days of prayer and preparation. The thirty-third day typically culminates in a formal Act of Consecration to Mary. By doing this act, the individual entrusts their body, soul, works, and entire life to Our Lady's loving care and intercession. Marian consecration is an incredibly meaningful and transformative spiritual practice that can bring immense grace and blessings to our lives. St. Louis de Montfort wrote *"The True Devotion to Mary."*

To complete the Consecration to the Immaculate Heart of Mary, the final day must be celebrated on one of the Marian feasts that the faithful are most devoted to. To carry out the consecration, we can choose a date from the main celebrations of the Marian Calendar, count back 33 days, and take that day as the official beginning of the consecration. At the end of the 33 days, we must receive confession and communion and perform the act of consecration before an image of the Virgin. The consecration should be signed on the same day as a symbol of our commitment to our Mother and God. It is recommended to perform an act of mercy, like fasting, mortification, or almsgiving, on that day to show our gratitude and commitment. This consecration can deepen our faith, enhance our spiritual journey, and strengthen our relationship with Mary and God.

Frequency:
This consecration can be renewed every year.

DEVOTION to the Saints

As we seek to lead a holy life, it is suggested that we select a favorite saint to act as a permanent spiritual guide and mentor. This Saint can be someone who resonates with us and whose life and teachings inspire us to be better versions of ourselves. We can also choose a different saint each month to invoke their help and seek their intercession in our prayers. In addition, we can celebrate and honor the Saint of the day according to the liturgical calendar of our Catholic Church, recognizing their virtues and seeking to emulate their example. By seeking the guidance and inspiration of the Saints, we can draw closer to God and grow in holiness.

As they stand before God, The Saints eagerly await our petitions. They are our lawyers, representing us before God. Through the merits of Jesus and the power of God, they intercede for us to obtain blessings and graces that we may not be able to get on our own. How many graces would they love to pour out on us if we only ask them for help? Let's take advantage of each of them.

MY PERMANENT SAINT I pray to is:_____
   My Saint of this month is:_____
   Today we honor Saint:_____

FREQUENCY:
Invoke the help of the Saints daily.

. . .

The Angelus

The Angelus is a beautiful prayer that celebrates the incarnation of Jesus and is considered a powerful devotion in the Catholic faith. It is traditionally repeated three times a day at specific times: 6 a.m., 12 p.m., and 6 p.m., inviting us to pause and reflect on our faith.

Initially, the Angelus was meant to be recited on one's knees and to the sound of church bells, adding an extra layer of reverence and devotion to the prayer. However, Pope Leo XIII later modified it to be less rigorous, allowing people to pray at any time during the mornings, around noon, and in the evenings while respecting the specific hours whenever possible. If we forget to recite the complete prayer, we can replace it with 5 Hail Marys. It is also worth noting that reciting the Angelus comes with a partial indulgence.

The Chaplet of Divine Mercy

Jesus revealed this devotion of mercy to St. Faustina Kowalska. Diary 1541

> "Encourage souls to say the Chaplet which I have given you. Whoever will recite it will receive great mercy at the hour of death. When they say this Chaplet in the presence of the dying, I will stand between My Father and the dying person, not as the just Judge but as the Merciful Savior. Priests will recommend it to sinners as their last hope of salvation. Even if there were a sinner most hardened, if he were to recite this Chaplet only once, he would receive grace from My infinite mercy. I desire to grant unimaginable graces to those souls who trust in My mercy. Through the Chaplet you will obtain

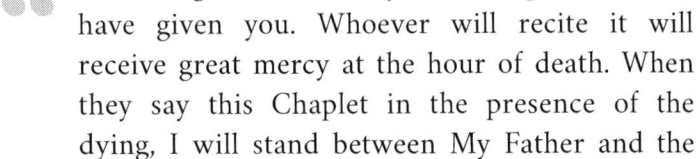

everything, if what you ask for is compatible with My will."[1]

The Chaplet of Divine Mercy is a prayer that can be recited at any time using the traditional beads of the Rosary. It is a powerful prayer that the Lord specifically revealed to St. Faustina, who instructed her to recite it as a novena during the nine days leading up to the Feast of Mercy. The Feast of Mercy is celebrated on the first Sunday after Easter and is a special day of grace and forgiveness. The Lord promised that those who recite the Chaplet of Divine Mercy as a novena during this time will be granted all possible graces. This promise is recorded in the Diary of St. Faustina, which is a testament to the Lord's great love and mercy for all of humanity.

Diary of St. Faustina, 796

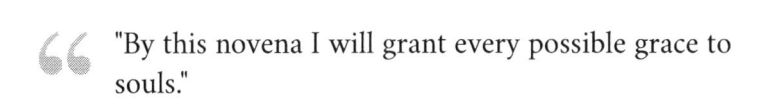

> "By this novena I will grant every possible grace to souls."

This sacred devotion revolves around the time when Jesus Christ breathed his last breath, which was at 3 p.m. Jesus promised St. Faustina that whoever practices this devotion will be granted whatever they ask.

> Diary of St. Faustina, 1320
> "At three o'clock, implore My mercy, especially for sinners; and, if only for a brief moment, immerse yourself in My Passion, particularly in My abandonment at the moment of agony. This is the hour of great mercy for the whole world. I will allow you to enter into My mortal sorrow. In this

hour, I will refuse nothing to the soul that makes a request of Me in virtue of My Passion."[2]

Diary, 1572

"I remind you, My daughter, that as often as you hear the clock strike the third hour, immerse yourself completely in My mercy, adoring and glorifying it; invoke its omnipotence for the whole world, and particularly for poor sinners; for at that moment mercy was opened wide for every soul. In this hour you can obtain everything for yourself and for others for the asking; it was the hour of grace for the whole world-mercy triumphed over justice." [3]

Prayers for The Hour of Great Mercy
At three o'clock in the afternoon we must recite the following prayer:

(*Diary of St. Faustina Kowalska, 1319*)
"You expired, Jesus, but the source of life gushed forth for souls,
and the ocean of mercy opened up for the whole world.
O Fount of Life, unfathomable Divine Mercy,
envelop the whole world and empty yourself out upon us."
[4]

Repeat three times:
(Diary, 84)

"O Blood and Water, which gushed forth from the

Heart of Jesus as a fountain of Mercy for us, I trust in you!"[5]

We can Pray in a chapel, meditating on Christ's Passion, especially his agony.

Divine Mercy Sunday

Divine Mercy Sunday is the first Sunday after Easter. This is a day of great significance because of Jesus's promise to us through the revelations to Saint Faustina. This promise is nothing short of extraordinary, as it is a grace that is simpler and more accessible than a plenary indulgence. It is like a second Baptism, as it washes away all our sins and their consequences. This means that we will be responsible only for any sins we commit after this day, but it also means that our souls will be renewed and restored to a state of purity, just like a newborn baby. It is a day of hope and renewal when we can begin afresh with a clean slate through the mercy of God. Every catholic should practice this devotion.

LET'S READ JESUS PROMISES:

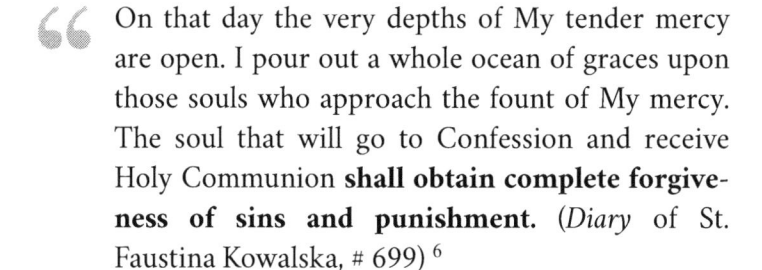

> On that day the very depths of My tender mercy are open. I pour out a whole ocean of graces upon those souls who approach the fount of My mercy. The soul that will go to Confession and receive Holy Communion **shall obtain complete forgiveness of sins and punishment.** (*Diary* of St. Faustina Kowalska, # 699) [6]

To receive the grace, we need to fulfill two essential conditions.

- Firstly, we must go to Sacramental Confession within 20 days before or after Divine Mercy Sunday. This helps us renew our friendship with God. It is recommended that we go to confession a day before Divine Mercy Sunday to keep ourselves as close as possible to a state of grace.
- Secondly, we must take the Eucharistic communion at the Divine Mercy Sunday mass.

*By fulfilling these two conditions, we can receive the grace and blessings of the Divine Mercy Sunday.

Jesus requested that we also do works of mercy, such as good deeds or prayers. We can participate in the Divine Mercy devotions that day or say, "Jesus, I trust in you," three times.

THE LITURGY of the Hours (Divine Office)

The Liturgy of the Hours is an ancient practice of the Catholic Church that has been carried out for centuries. It is a set of daily prayers that are recited at specific times throughout the day, with the intention of sanctifying each day with prayer.

The Liturgy of the Hours is a communal prayer recited by Catholics worldwide. While the recitation of the Liturgy of the Hours is mandatory for priests by canon law, the laity is not required to participate. However, the Church recommends that we do so, as it is a powerful way to connect with God and one another. The laity may choose to recite the prayers of Lauds and Vespers at a minimum, as these prayers are typically recited in the morning and evening. Let's read the Catechism of the Church 1196 in this regard:

> #1196 "The faithful who celebrate the Liturgy of the Hours are united to Christ, our High Priest, by the prayer of the Psalms, the meditation on the

Word of God, the songs and the blessings, to be associated with his unceasing and universal prayer that gives glory to the Father and implores the gift of the Holy Spirit upon the whole world."[7]

Canon law 1174:

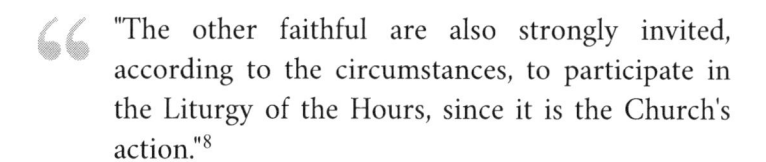

> "The other faithful are also strongly invited, according to the circumstances, to participate in the Liturgy of the Hours, since it is the Church's action."[8]

Pope John Paul II, in his apostolic letter of December 4, 2003, tells us the following:

> "It is important to introduce the faithful to the celebration of the Liturgy of the Hours, which, as the public prayer of the Church, is a source of piety and nourishment for personal prayer. It is not an individual or private action, but belongs to the whole body of the Church. Therefore, when the faithful are summoned and gather for the Liturgy of the Hours, uniting their hearts and their voices, they make visible the Church, which celebrates the mystery of Christ. This privileged attention to liturgical prayer is not in opposition to personal prayer; on the contrary, it presupposes and demands it, and it harmonizes very well with other forms of community prayer, especially if they have been recognized and recommended by ecclesial authority" (14).[9]

The Apostolic Constitutions of the 2nd-3rd century recommended to Christians:

> "You must pray in the morning, at the third, sixth, ninth, and evening hours, and at the crowing of the cock."

Benedict Monks Practiced These Prayers

The monks had a strict prayer routine, which included reciting all 150 Psalms in the Psalter each week. The "minor hours" of prayer did not require them to go to church, but as soon as they heard the trumpet or bell, the monks would stop whatever they were doing and begin to pray, no matter where they were. For the "major hours" of prayer, which included matins, lauds, and vespers, the entire community would gather in the church. These were the most essential prayer times, and the monks would come together to chant the Psalms and offer their prayers to God.

> "Lay groups gathering for prayer, apostolic work, or any other reason are encouraged to fulfill the Church's duty by celebrating part of the liturgy of the hours. The laity must learn, above all, how, in the liturgy, they are adoring God the Father in spirit and truth; they should bear in mind that through public worship and prayer, they reach all humanity and can contribute significantly to the salvation of the whole world.
>
> … it is of great advantage for the family, the domestic sanctuary of the Church, not only to pray together to God but also to celebrate some parts of the liturgy of the hours as occasion offers, in order to enter more deeply into the life of the Church."
>
> *General Instruction of the Liturgy of the Hours,* Congregation for Divine Worship[10]

INDULGENCES

Indulgences are a significant element of our faith and play a crucial role in the journey towards holiness. Indulgences are an infallible part of the Church's teachings, which means that every Catholic is obliged to believe in them. The Council of Trent, an ecumenical council that took place in the 16th century, condemned with anathema anyone who claimed that indulgences are useless or that the Church lacks the power to grant them. Let's read:

COUNCIL OF TRENT, session 25 decrees of indulgences:

> "Whereas the power of conferring Indulgences was granted by Christ to the Church; and she has, even in the most ancient times, used the said power, delivered unto her of God; the sacred holy Synod teaches, and enjoins, that the use of Indulgences, for the Christian people most salutary, and approved of by the authority of sacred Councils, is to be retained in the Church; and It condemns with anathema those who either assert, that they are useless ; or who deny that there is in the Church the power of granting them…"[11]

With indulgences, we can obtain the remission of the temporal punishment due to the consequences of our sins. We can also obtain this mercy for the souls in purgatory.

The practice of making atonement for the death originated in the early Church and is based on the same scriptures.

> *2 Maccabees 12:46:*
> *" It is therefore a holy and wholesome thought to pray for the dead, that they may be loosed from sins.."*

Praying for the Dead is one of the seven spiritual works of mercy:
1. Teach those who do not know
2. Give good advice to those who need it
3. Correct the one who is in error
4. Forgive injuries
5. Comfort the sad
6. Suffer defects with patience
7, *Pray to God for the living and the deceased.

Why do we need to pray for the deceased?

It's an act of mercy because we are one of the reasons they ended up in purgatory. Our actions and words can influence others to sin and be negatively affected by its consequences. Whether it is through giving bad advice or setting a bad example, we have the power to impact the lives of those around us. Therefore, it is important that we are mindful of our behavior and strive to be a positive influence on those we interact with. When a person sins, he acquires consequences of guilt and punishment. Even the smallest sins are subject to God's justice:

> *Ecclesiastes 12:14:*
> *"And all things that are done, God will bring into judgment for every error, whether it be good or evil."*

We know that some punishments have eternal consequences, but there are also temporal consequences:

> *Genesis 3:16*
> *"16 To the woman also he said: I will multiply thy sorrows, and thy conceptions: in sorrow shalt thou bring forth children, and thou shalt be under thy*

THE PATH TO HOLINESS

> husband's power, and he shall have dominion over thee."

even if the sin is forgiven, there are still temporary penalties. we see this clearly in 2 Samuel 12:13:

> "And David said to Nathan: I have sinned against the Lord. And Nathan said to David: The Lord also hath taken away thy sin: thou shalt not die.
> ¹⁴ Nevertheless, because thou hast given occasion to the enemies of the Lord to blaspheme, for this thing, the child that is born to thee, shall surely die."

In this passage, God forgave David for his sins, but David still had to suffer the loss of his son.

What does the Catechism of the Catholic Church 1471 tell us:

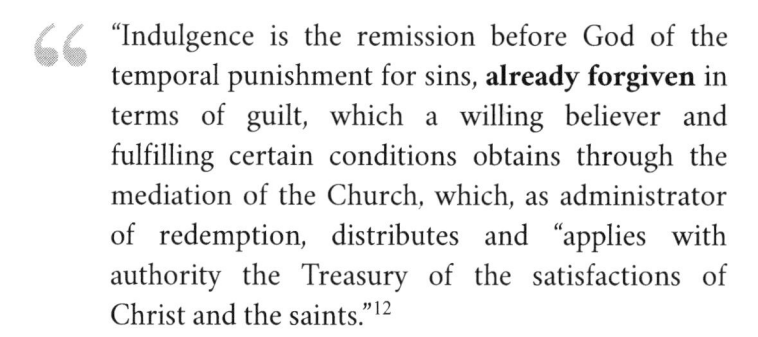

> "Indulgence is the remission before God of the temporal punishment for sins, **already forgiven** in terms of guilt, which a willing believer and fulfilling certain conditions obtains through the mediation of the Church, which, as administrator of redemption, distributes and "applies with authority the Treasury of the satisfactions of Christ and the saints."[12]

In other words:

Indulgence erases the consequences of our sins ALREADY FORGIVEN THROUGH CONFESSION. Let's read what Jesus said to Saint Faustina:

> (Diary of Saint Faustina #1226):
> "Today bring to Me the souls who are in the

prison of Purgatory, and immerse them in the abyss of My mercy. Let the torrents of My Blood cool down their scorching flames. All these souls are greatly loved by Me. They are making retribution to My justice. It is in your power to bring them relief. Draw all the indulgences from the treasury of My Church and offer them on their behalf. Oh, if you only knew the torments they suffer, you would continually offer for them the alms of the spirit and pay off their debt to My justice."[13]

Indulgences can help believers shorten or completely eliminate their time in purgatory. However, obtaining indulgences is challenging, as it requires fulfilling four important requirements. Most notably, a believer must be completely detached from all sins, even minor ones. Due to the strict nature of these requirements, many indulgences become partial, and it is impossible to know whether they have been accepted.

Indulgences can help the faithful ascend to Heaven in a much shorter period than deserved. In some cases, it may even help us avoid purgatory altogether. Let's read Saint Teresa of the Child Jesus:

> "One day, Saint Teresa of Jesús saw, full of joy, that the soul of a nun who had just died ascended radiantly to Heaven. This nun had a very normal life, nothing extraordinary. Our Lord Jesus Christ explained to her the reason for such a privilege: "She always had great confidence in the indulgences granted by the Church; and she always strove to win as many as possible."

Indulgences are a way for the Church to offer us spiritual

wealth and reduce the punishment that one might have to endure in purgatory. Therefore, we must take advantage of them as much as possible if we want to grow in virtue and avoid purgatory.

MORTIFICATIONS

The term "mortification" has an etymology originating from the Latin words "mors," which means death, and "facere," which means to do. Together, they signify "To bring about death." This word can be used in various contexts, such as referring to the physical decay of a body or the emotional distress caused by a humiliating experience. Despite its negative connotations, the word mortification can also suggest a sense of humility and self-reflection, as it reminds us of our mortality. In mortification, we kill our sinful habits for the purification of the soul.

Types of Mortification

Mortification is a practice of self-discipline that involves inflicting physical or psychological suffering on oneself for the purpose of spiritual purification. There are two types of mortification: passive and active:

- Passive mortification involves accepting unprovoked everyday suffering. This can take many forms, such as accidentally hitting one's knee, experiencing humiliation, or losing a family member. While passive mortification is not actively sought out, it is still viewed as a means of purifying the soul by accepting suffering humbly and patiently.
- Active mortification, on the other hand, is the conscious pursuit of suffering and the use of it as a tool for salvation. Examples of active mortification

include fasting, penance, denial of carnal pleasures, and self-flagellation.

Mortification plays an important role in the journey towards holiness. Mortification is an essential aspect of our spiritual discipline, as it helps us to develop humility and submit our flesh to the Spirit. Through mortification, we learn to be more compassionate towards the suffering of humanity as we become more attuned to our pains and weaknesses. This practice also helps us master our temptations as we learn to resist the allure of pleasure and self-indulgence. By accepting and offering our mortifications to God, we can pay for the consequences of our sins and shorten our time in purgatory. This act of self-denial can also help us to grow in virtue and save souls as we develop greater discipline and self-control.

CORPORAL MORTIFICATIONS in Today's World

Mortifications applied to spiritual growth are often criticized as fanaticism or madness in modern times. As human beings, we have an inherent aversion to pain and suffering, and yet, with the help of divine grace, we can learn to accept and even overcome these difficult experiences. However, the problem arises when we use this ability to overcome suffering for personal and selfish gains. When we use our mortifications as a spiritual growth and tool for salvation, we are often misunderstood and stigmatized as being fanatical or even crazy.

The rejection of self-mortification for Christ seems hypocritical when we consider that mortification is already practiced for personal and vain purposes. Unfortunately, those who choose to mortify themselves for Christ may be labeled as "masochists." This hypocrisy is evident in the practice of euthanasia, where individuals choose to end their lives for selfish reasons, merely to alleviate their own suffering. Similarly, cosmetic surgeries can be painful, requiring cuts, bruises, fasting, and days of bed rest, all for the sole purpose of improving one's physical appearance and feeding the self. Strict diets and denying oneself to lose weight are other examples. Even tattoos can be painful, yet people still choose to endure the pain for the sake of their appearance. It is important to consider the motives behind self-mortification and to recognize that it can be a means of offering oneself as an instrument of salvation.

Let's talk about the daredevils who climb Mount Everest. Despite the bitterly cold conditions, many risk their lives to achieve their goal or make a statement. Unfortunately, some of these adventurers do not make it back alive, and their mummified bodies are left spread across the mountain like jerky meat. While some may see these individuals as heroes or brave, their loved ones are left behind to suffer, with debts and everything else that entitles the loss of a family member. Clap, clap, clap. How selfish.

While our intention is not to demonize mountaineers, it's important to understand that the careless pursuit of extreme sports done for selfish reasons is a form of vain mortification.

It's difficult to ignore the sexual games played by fornicators who engage in practices such as flogging themselves with whips, pulling their hair, or walking on their knees while being humiliated with a dog collar. What's more concerning is that these activities are deemed 'normal' and acceptable. Ah! the hypocrisy.

It's unfortunate that in our society, acts of selfishness are often celebrated, admired, and seen as exemplary. However, the story is quite different regarding acts of faith. If a person of faith chooses to fast to honor God, they could be ridiculed and labeled as "fanatics." Similarly, if a faithful person decides to engage in self-flagellation to save souls, it is seen as scandalous and labeled as "crazy," "masochistic," or worse. It's an example of the hypocrisy of our society.

Mortification in Scriptures

Mortification is a practice that has been prevalent since the beginning of Christianity. Early Christians are known to have given up their lives for Christ, which is the ultimate form of mortification. In the Old Testament, we see people engaging in various mortifying practices, such as fasting, dressing in sackcloth, and putting ashes on their heads to express repentance and seek divine intervention.

The second person of the Holy Trinity, Jesus Christ, took on human form and suffered for us. He came to this earth to endure immense pain and mortified himself for the sake of humanity. Despite being blameless, He was subjected to ridicule, torture, and crucifixion for our sins. If Jesus could undergo such intense suffering for our salvation, why can't we mortify ourselves for Christ? The Saints definitely agree.

Saint Jacinta, one of the three children who witnessed the apparitions of the Virgin Mary in Fatima, had a deep devotion to the salvation of souls. She would often tie a rough rope around her waist, which caused her significant discomfort, pain, and bleeding to the point of tears. Despite the suffering, she willingly endured it as a sacrifice for the conversion of sinners, offering her pain to God as a way to help others turn away from sin.

Let's see if the Virgin Mary told her she was a fanatic masochist:

> "Our Lord is very happy with your sacrifices, but He does not want you to sleep on the rope. Wear it only during the day."

Saint Rose of Lima slept on a wooden bed without a mattress, wore a silver crown with spikes hidden by roses on her head, and had an iron chain around her waist, among other practices. It was well known that Pope John Paul II practiced flogging. Cardinal José Saraiva stated when asked about the self-mortification of the Holy Pope:

> "It looks like something from another era, but it's not. It is an instrument of perfection, not only in religious life but in human life."

> "Whenever a person wants to achieve excellence, sacrifice is necessary," the cardinal said. Whether one seeks holiness or excellence at work or in sports, he said, "it demands self-denial, extraordinary efforts."

Sᴛ. Catherine of Siena wore a sackcloth (instrument of mortification) and flogged herself three times a day in imitation of St. Dominic. Padre Pio of Pietrelcina, the Saint who received the stigmata, wrote in one of his letters:

> "Let us now consider what we must do to make the Holy Spirit dwell in our souls. It can all be **summed up in the mortification of the flesh**. with its vices and lusts, and in protection against a selfish spirit... **Mortification should be constant and constant**, not intermittent, and **should last a lifetime**. Moreover, the perfect Christian must not be content with a kind of mortification. which just seems to be severe. **You have to make sure it hurts.**"

St. Francis de Sales also flogged himself; Mother Teresa of

Calcutta chose to live in extreme poverty and also flogged herself. As St. Alphonsus says, penance and mortification are necessary to "*restrain the inordinate inclinations of self-love.*"

MESSAGE of Our Lady of Fatima:

> "Sacrifice yourself for sinners, and say many times, especially when you make a sacrifice: O Jesus, it is for love of You, for the conversion of sinners and in reparation for sins committed against the Immaculate Heart of Mary."
> 14

St. Alphonsus de Ligouri:

> "If we read the lives of the saints and see the works of penance they performed, we will be ashamed of the delicacy and reserve with which we punish the flesh... Our pilgrimage on earth will not be of long duration: our abode is eternity, where he who has practiced the greatest mortifications during life will enjoy the greatest glory."

These mortifications should be practiced with measure without causing permanent damage or danger to life. Mortifying oneself, for Christ, is an act of love.

> Catechism of the Catholic Church 2289
>
> "**2289** Morality demands respect for bodily life, but it does not make it an absolute value. It is opposed to a neo-pagan conception that tends to promote the *cult of the body*, to sacrifice everything

to it, to idolize physical perfection and sporting success. Such a conception, because of the selection that operates between the strong and the weak, can lead to the perversion of human relations."[15]

MODERATE MORTIFICATION for the salvation of souls was and remained for more than 2,000 years an instrument of perfection in the way of holiness. The Catholic Church does not forbid mortification, and in the case of rigorous mortifications, advises that it be done through a spiritual director.

SOME INSTRUMENTS of Mortification

- Cilice: A cilice is a spiked chain worn around the upper thigh for two hours a day, except on Church holidays, Sundays, and certain times of the year.
- The Whip: used on the buttocks or back once a week.
- Bathing in cold water
- Sleeping without a mattress
- Practicing Silence
- Sleeping without a pillow
- Use salt instead of sugar in beverages
- Wearing a Crown of Thorns
- Walking on your knees
- Turn off Social media

Frequency:
Practice it at least once a month

DEVOTIONS to the Souls in Purgatory

Every person who seeks holiness understands the importance of helping the souls in purgatory. Without exception, every saint has cared for these souls. It is believed that attaining Heaven is not possible without offering our assistance to those in purgatory. Praying for them is a duty for every Catholic, as we have directly or indirectly contributed to many of these souls ending up there through our actions and their consequences. It is likely that we, too, will have to experience purgatory. Let's analyze a scenario:

Diane is a single mother who is 57 years old. She lives paycheck to paycheck and relies on the bus for transportation. One day, while she was asleep on the bus, she was robbed by a teenager named Bob, who was sitting next to her. If Bob were to pass away and face judgment from God, would he only be held accountable for the theft he committed against Diane? No, he would also be held accountable for the ripple effect that his actions caused and the consequences that resulted from it.

Let's continue:

After losing her money, Diane is unable to purchase her medication for chronic migraines, which causes her to become irritable and aggressive towards people, especially her children. She doesn't have enough money to buy food for her baby, resulting in the baby becoming sick. Her other children become stressed due to the lack of food. Taking the baby to the doctor results in an expensive medical bill she can't afford. Diane asks her neighbor to lend her money, but her neighbor refuses. As a result of her stressful situation, Diane mistreats her older children. They go to school in a bad mood and treat other children poorly. Bob the thief confesses his sins and receives absolution, believing that his sins are forgiven and that he will go straight to Heaven if he dies. However, he fails to make reparations for the consequences of his sin. His actions have created purgatory for himself, Diane, Diane's neighbor, her older children, and many others.

> These consequences of sin continue to leave traces and can only be healed with reparation.

The reality is that most of us will have to go through purgatory (if saved). The souls in purgatory are considered holy as they cannot commit any more sins but are in an imperfect spiritual state and require purification. However, they are ultimately saved and will one day see God. Each soul in purgatory is in harmony with God's will, accepting everything that happens on earth, good and bad. They understand that without God, nothing is possible and unite their will with his. It is our responsibility not only to pray for the souls of our loved ones but also for the souls of those whom God has placed in our lives.

St. Thomas Aquinas wrote that *"prayers for the dead are the most acceptable to God, because the dead have need of it and cannot help themselves like the living."*

How to Help the Souls in Purgatory

The Holy Sacrifice of the Mass is the most effective way to help the Souls in Purgatory reach paradise. One pious practice is the celebration of Gregorian Masses. These consist of a series of 30 Masses offered for the deceased without any interruption. The Masses are held as soon as possible after the person's death. It is believed that at the end of these Masses, the soul reaches Heaven or obtains a better spiritual state in purgatory. However, only God can determine this based on the debts of the soul. Since most parishes do not have the time to celebrate these Masses consecutively, they are usually held by monasteries.

A good practice is also to offer our communion for the benefit of the departed. Another practice involves adopting a group of souls in purgatory, which can include relatives, friends, or any individuals who have committed transgressions such as abortion, infidelity, suicide, or murder. We offer prayers and make sacrifices for that group of souls for a month. After a month, we switch to a different group until we have covered as many as possible, and then we start again. We can also take many souls out of purgatory with indulgences, prayers, sacrifices, and acts of charity.

IF WE OFFER ALL our prayers for the souls in purgatory, we will not have time to pray for ourselves
Not true. Praying for others is never wasted. St. Thomas Aquinas, in the "Summa Theologica" explains:

> "Satisfactory work does not only benefit those for whom it is intended; but much more to the one who does it" (Supplement 71, 5).

Frequency:
Practice pious devotions every day

* * *

AGREEMENT

Date:

Starting today, I will begin practicing the following devotions.

_____

Signature:

_____

17

STEP TWELVE

PRAYING ALL DAY LONG

The first commandment is the most important and the foundation of every commandment.

"You shall love the Lord your God with all your heart, and with all your soul and with all your strength."

Maintaining a daily line of communication with God is crucial. Prayer allows us to connect with Him, and by praising and adoring God, we unite ourselves to the source of life. Prayer is a constant practice that we are called to undertake every day.

> *1 Tesalonicenses 5:17-18*
> *[17] Pray without ceasing.*
> *[18] In all things give thanks; for this is the will of God in Christ Jesus concerning you all."*

Many people wonder how one can pray all day without feeling exhausted or losing interest. We picture ourselves on our knees, reciting long prayers without being able to move. There are many other ways to pray continuously throughout the day. One approach is to start the day by expressing gratitude to God as soon as we open our eyes. We can say,

"Blessed and praised are you, Lord, King of the Universe. Thank you for the precious gift of life."

As we go about our daily routine, we can continuously talk to the Lord and offer our actions as a prayer. For instance, while walking to the grocery store, we can thank the Lord for our legs and ask that they always lead us toward Him. We can also bless not only our food but everything that enters our mouths, saying,

"Thank you, Lord, for this water and this apple that comes from you."

when we purchase new clothes or shoes, we can thank the Lord for providing us with the means to obtain them. By making every action a form of prayer, we can constantly communicate with God throughout the day.

Often, we live our lives without giving much thought to God. We may only mention Him when we say phrases like "Oh my God," but this is usually just a figure of speech and not an actual conversation with God. To always keep Jesus in our thoughts, we can use an image of our Lord and bow to it every time we see it. This simple act can constantly remind us of His presence in our lives. We can also sing songs to Him, praising His glory and expressing gratitude for His love and mercy.

When we accidentally cut our hands in the kitchen or experience any other kind of pain, we can turn our suffering into a prayer and unite ourselves with those who need spiritual help. Practicing obedience and doing our homework without complaining is also a form of prayer.

St. Therese of the Child Jesus teaches us to do our daily work for the love of God:

> "It's not about doing big things; it's about doing the little things with great love."

We also pray when we do the right thing and set an example for others:

Matthew 5:14-16:

> "*¹⁴* You are the light of the world. A city seated on a mountain cannot be hid.
> *¹⁵* Neither do men light a candle and put it under a bushel, but upon a candlestick, that it may shine to all that are in the house.
> *¹⁶* So **let your light shine before men**, that they may see your good works, and glorify your Father who is in heaven."

Frequency:
Every day, all day, at all hours

* * *

AGREEMENT

Date:

Every morning, I will begin to praise my God and eventually commit to daily prayer.

Signature:
_____

18

STEP THIRTEEN

FASTING

Fasting is an effective practice in the pursuit of holiness. It enables us to control our physical desires and sharpen our focus on our spiritual journey. When we subject ourselves to fasting, our survival instincts kick in, and our body redirects its energy toward finding food, often reducing sinful thoughts and behavior.

When we feel hungry, our body enters survival mode. This means that our hunger is the only desire we need to overcome during fasting. By dominating the flesh, we can gain more control over our spirit. Fasting is a powerful and essential tool in our journey towards achieving holiness.

> *Matthew 17:20*
> *"[20] But this kind is not cast out but by prayer and fasting."*

DAYS OF FASTING AND ABSTINENCE

Ash Wednesday and Good Friday are mandatory days of fasting

and abstinence for Catholics. Fridays during Lent are obligatory days of abstinence. We should also fast every Friday of the year.

What does the Code of Canon Law tell us?

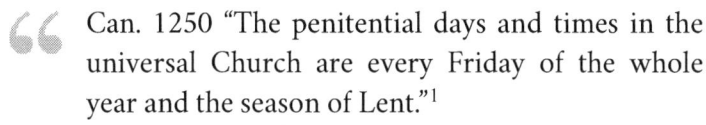

> Can. 1250 "The penitential days and times in the universal Church are every Friday of the whole year and the season of Lent."[1]
>
> Can. 1251 "Abstinence from meat, or from some other food as determined by the Episcopal Conference, is to be observed on **all Fridays**, unless a solemnity should fall on a Friday. Abstinence and fasting are to be observed on Ash Wednesday and Good Friday."[2]

When fasting, a person is allowed to eat one full meal a day and two smaller meals that together do not equal a full meal.

Abstinence consists of not eating meat. On Ash Wednesday and Good Friday, there are days of abstinence and fasting (both in one day). All those between the ages of 18 and 59 are required to fast. Abstinence is mandatory from the age of 14.

FASTING ACCORDING TO OUR LADY IN MEDJUGORJE

Message of our Lady on August 14, 1984:

> "...Fast strictly on Wednesdays and Fridays..."

By fasting and prayer, we can change the world:

> December 25, 1982, to Mirjana, ..."You have forgotten that through prayer and fasting you can avert wars **and suspend the laws of nature**.[3]

Our Lady asks us to fast without going hungry, substituting the usual three meals for only bread and water.

> July 21, 1982 "...The best fast is on bread and water. Through fasting and prayer, one **can stop wars, one can suspend the laws of nature**. Charity cannot replace fasting...everyone, except the sick, must fast."[4]

In the canons of St. Peter of Alexandria, a martyr, we can read the following about fasting on Wednesdays and Fridays:

> "Let no one find us in default of fasting on Wednesdays and Fridays, according to the custom so well dictated by tradition: Wednesday because of the judgment of the Jews and the betrayal of the Lord, and Friday because of all that He suffered for us."

The Medjugorje fast should begin in the morning and continue for twenty-four hours the next day. Fasting is not only physical but also spiritual. We can fast from our vices, such as not using social media for a day, not swearing, etc.

Frequency:

Fasting must be part of our path to holiness. We should practice it weekly at least once a week.

AGREEMENT

Date:

Today, I pledge to fast regularly every:

☐ Week

☐ Month

Signature:

_____

STEP FOURTEEN

HOME ALTAR AND THE USE OF SACRAMENTALS

THE ALTAR

Our homes are considered an extension of the Church. It is recommended that every Catholic family have an altar in their home, which serves as a sacred place to worship God. On this altar, we can keep our Bible, holy images of the Virgin Mary and the Saints, a crucifix, and other important sacramentals.

The altar is a sacred place for prayer and meditation. It is an extension of the church inside our homes, where we come together to connect with God as a family. We must enter our altar with reverence and respect, whether by bowing or making the sign of the cross. Our altar serves as a refuge where we can escape whenever we have problems. It's also helpful to have a chair on our altar where we can sit, talk to God, and pour out our hearts to Him, just as we do when we go to the Blessed Sacrament.

We read the Bible at our altar, practice our devotions, and pray the rosary. We continue to pray for our deceased loved ones, those who are ill, and our relatives. Through our intercessory prayers, we also help the world. Our Altar shines like a diamond, and it's seen from Heaven.

ALTAR LOCATION

Every Catholic Church is located facing the East. This is because we believe that Jesus will return from the East at His Second Coming

> *Matthew 24:27:*
> *²⁷ For as lightning cometh out of the east, and appeareth even into the west: so shall the coming of the Son of man be."*

Our altar should be placed (preferably) on the east side of our house. We achieve this by using a Compass. Once the east side of that wall is located, we set up our altar right there.

THE SACRAMENTALS

In the early days of Christianity, most people were illiterate and did not have personal Bibles; the church understood this and found ways to bring the faith to Christians through icons, images, and other objects known as sacramentals. These sacramentals are blessed objects and include exorcisms intended to drive out evil spirits, although sacramental confession is believed to be even more powerful.

Sacramentals are also relics, objects sanctified through the life of a saint or martyr. They are designed to prepare us for the sacraments and are deeply rooted in the Bible.

Let us remember the woman who touched the Lord's tunic and was healed in Matthew 9:20:

> "*²⁰ And behold a woman who was troubled with an issue of blood twelve years, came behind him, and touched the hem of his garment.*
> *²¹ For she said within herself: If I shall touch only his garment, I shall be healed.*
> *²² But Jesus turning and seeing her, said: Be of good heart, daughter, thy faith hath made thee whole. And the woman was made whole from that hour."*

ANOTHER EXAMPLE IS Acts 19:11:

> "*¹¹ God did extraordinary miracles through Paul, ¹² so that when the **handkerchiefs or aprons that had touched his skin** were brought to the sick, **their diseases left them, and the evil spirits came out of them.***"

The use of holy water so criticized by the sects is in the Bible:

> Numbers 5:17:
> "*¹⁷ And he shall take **holy water** in an earthen vessel, and he shall cast a little earth of the pavement of the tabernacle into it."*

Sacramentals are sacred objects that prepare individuals to receive the grace of God. These objects are not sacraments themselves, but they lead the faithful to the sacraments and help them to receive them accordingly. Examples of sacramentals include holy water, candles, and scapulars.

It is important to note that the effectiveness of sacramentals cannot be guaranteed, as it depends on the faith of the individual who uses them. Sacramentals are not lucky charms; it is the faith of the individual that makes them effective and transformative. The sacramentals won't have the proper effect if we are not in a state of grace. Sacramentals obtain graces through Jesus's sacrifice on the cross. They do not have graces of their own and are authorized by the Church because she has the power to do so.

USING SACRAMENTALS

Sacramentals are the tools the Church provides us to help us maintain the graces we receive from the sacraments and protect ourselves from the enemy. They are similar to the medicine a sick person takes home to continue healing after leaving the hospital. It is essential for every Catholic to keep their sacramentals blessed and use them at all times. They should not be treated as mere decorations but as objects of faith that deserve veneration and help us receive God's grace.

We can use many types of sacramentals, including holy water, blessed salt, votive candles, medals, oils, rosaries, scapulars, and more. Each of these items has a specific purpose and helps us obtain graces.

It is important to use sacramentals regularly. For instance, we bless ourselves with holy water before entering or leaving our house. We also bless our house and our family. When we pray at our Altar, we light votive candles. Occasionally, we purify our home with previously blessed incense. For protection, we place the Saint Benedict medal in each room.

WHAT DOES the Catechism of the Catholic Church say in 1667

> "1667 "Holy Mother Church has, moreover, instituted sacramentals. These are sacred signs which bear a resemblance to the sacraments. They signify effects, particularly of a spiritual nature, which are

obtained through the intercession of the Church. By them men are disposed to receive the chief effect of the sacraments, and various occasions in life are rendered holy."[1]

Frequency:
Use the Sacramentals daily

* * *

AGREEMENT

Date:

Today, I commit to pray at my home altar every:

☐ Day

☐ Week

and, if I haven't already, I'll start using my sacramentals.

Signature:

_____

20

THE FRUITS OF HOLINESS

What are the effects of walking toward holiness? How can we be sure we're on the right path, and what are the fruits of holiness?

As we walk the path of holiness, the fruits of the Holy Spirit begin to emerge and grow within us. Every soul is a masterpiece, and at the moment of creation, it is equipped with its own set of qualities, gifts, and talents. For example, some are born with the ability to sing, while others may be good at math, and others excel in certain sports. Some are born with the gift of forgiveness or humor, and others are naturally detached from worldly things. These gifts and talents are given to us at the moment our soul is created.

Furthermore, we receive other kinds of blessings through baptism, which are further sealed during the sacrament of confirmation. These are known as the gifts of the Holy Spirit. These gifts are infused within our souls and are activated as we grow in virtue and holiness by choosing to follow God's path.

Let's take a look at the seven gifts of the Holy Spirit:

The seven gifts of the Holy Spirit are:

- Wisdom, understanding, counsel, strength, knowledge, piety, and fear of God

Some certain qualities and characteristics grow in our souls by living according to the will of God, often without realizing it. This is called the fruits of the Holy Spirit, which are 12:

1. charity
2. Joy
3. Peace
4. Patience
5. Kindness
6. Goodness
7. Generosity
8. Gentleness
9. Faithfulness
10. Modesty
11. Self-Control
12. Chastity

SOME MANIFESTATIONS OF THE HOLY SPIRIT ON OUR PATH TO HOLINESS

DISCOVERING GOD IN ALL HIS CREATION

As we advance towards the Path of Holiness we will see the world through a different lens, As if a veil has been lifted. What was once mundane and ordinary now feels extraordinary and wonderful. Stepping out into the world, we observe the Heaven above and the beauty of its colors and clouds, and we cannot help but marvel at the work of God. The skinny and dry tree that we pass by every day now seems to be a masterpiece of art, its branches, leaves, and colors creating a symphony of beauty. The buzzing bees and singing birds, the green grass growing, all come together in a harmonious display of creation that reminds us of the presence of God in everything.

Everything that was once ignored and overlooked is now filled with deep meaning and appreciation as we become aware that God created everything for our benefit. We acknowledge the immense power of His creation and our insignificance. What used to seem plain and simple now acquires a whole new dimension in our consciousness. We observe our hands and analyze our body, noticing how each organ has a specific function that works in perfect harmony with the rest of our body. This intricate design shows God's presence everywhere in His creation. In the past, we were oblivious to this world without noticing the beauty around us. However, now we see everything in a new light and appreciate every little detail with amazement.

As described in 2 Corinthians 3:16

*"16 But when they shall be converted to the Lord, **the veil shall be taken away.***

As we go about our daily lives, it's easy to forget that God creates everything we enjoy and rely on in this world. Take a simple apple, for example. We eat it without a second thought, but it comes from a plant God created. The same is true of the cotton that makes our clothes. Where does the cotton comes from? From a plant. Who created the plants? God. the butter we spread on our bread comes from milk obtained from cows that God lovingly created.

God also created the very metals and rocks that make up the world around us. Think about the aluminum in the bike you ride. Its primary source is bauxite, a rock. Who created rocks? God. Everything comes from God. This appreciation of God's creation also leads us to develop a deeper appreciation for others. After all, we are all part of the same amazing work of God.

APRECIATION FOR PEOPLE

As we observe the magnificence of God's creation, it is impossible to limit our care and concern to only our family, friends, and those who benefit us. We tend to view others as "someone else's problem." But as we journey towards holiness, the Holy Spirit will open our eyes to see our fellow humans in a new light. We will begin to understand the amazing work of God in all humanity and recognize that He uniquely created each of us with His own breath (Genesis 2:7). This breath of God animates our being and gives us life. The same breath leaves our body when we die. It is a deep exhale that marks the end of our earthly journey, serving as a reminder that every human carries a part of God within themselves.

> Psalm 104:29
> *²⁹ When you hide your face, they are dismayed;*
> **when you take away their breath, they die**
> **and return to their dust.."**

> Psalm 146:4
> *"When* **their breath departs, they return to the earth;**
> *on that very day their plans perish."*

As we look at others with the eyes of the Spirit, we will be able to see the divine presence within them. Every human being is a breath of God walking through this world. When we understand this, we realize why we are so precious in the eyes of God. The second person of the Trinity left his throne and became one of us, mere flesh and blood. We understand why every soul and every human being is precious to Jesus. We are precious to Jesus because a piece of His Father exists within us. We comprehend the importance of the Second Commandment - "Love thy ncighbor as thyself" - and the gravity of not forgiving.

Walking down the street, we may find someone who catches our attention. In that moment, we may realize how much love our creator put into molding that person and how much the Lord desires that soul. how can we ever think that we are better than others or cannot forgive them? We can see the beauty in their skin, their eyes, and even their sense of humor. God's signature is all over us. Our bodies scream the greatness of God; that is why the sin of abortion is so abominable, for it involves the destruction of the very image and likeness of the living God. We are destroying the pot of clay that holds his precious breath. Abortion has devastating consequences that will affect generations to come.

As we journey through life, we gradually become more aware of the people around us. Our love for our neighbors grows daily, and soon, we find ourselves praying for those around us, even those who are not related to us in any way. We'd find ourselves praying for the person who had a car accident on the news, the waitress who served us in the restaurant, the ice cream man, and the barber. Suddenly, we realize that strangers matter to us. We want everyone to be saved, reach the Heavenly house, and experience the joy of eternal life. This precious gift of the Holy Spirit fills our hearts with compassion and love for God's creation. This newly found appreciation for humanity leads us to another manifestation: the spirit of Service.

THE SPIRIT OF SERVICE

When our spiritual eyes are open, we become more aware of the needs of others that we may have previously overlooked. We realize that we are all children of God and that every human being carries his breath. As a result, we feel compelled to serve and help others.

For example, we often overlook small details when we visit the grocery store. For instance, we might not notice a lady struggling to carry her bags. We might have ignored her in the past, thinking it was not our problem or someone else would help her. But now, things are different. We are more attentive to the needs of others. We keep an eye out for opportunities to be of service and to make a difference. And when we help someone, we do so gladly and willingly because, through them, we serve God.

THE FEAR OF GOD AND REJECTION OF SIN

By Recognizing the value of a human being, we now truly understand that when we offend our neighbor, we offend God. We see this from a profound perspective as we become aware of the gravity of our actions and the responsibility that comes with them. The Lord's Prayer establishes a condition for us to be forgiven.:

> "He forgives our trespasses "just as we forgive those who trespass against us."

> 66 Simply put, God won't forgive us if we don't forgive others.

We must forgive if we want to join God in Heaven. There is no way out, no shortcuts. Why? Because God's essence is love, and the only way to get to Him is through perfect love. As human beings, it is impossible for us to love God perfectly because of our sinful nature. However, we can love another human being perfectly, and this perfect love pleases God.

The fear of God does not arise from the threat of punishment or the fear of God's wrath but rather is rooted in our love for Him. It is a fear of being objects of disappointment and ungratefulness—a holy fear, if you will.

The fear of disappointing God goes hand in hand with the pain caused by sinning. We often try hard to obey Him, which hurts us deeply when we fail. Sometimes, we feel so disappointed in ourselves to the point of shedding tears. We fail our Lord like Peter did when he denied Him (Luke 22:54). Before embarking on our journey towards holiness, we used to sin without any remorse. Now, even the slightest sin hurts.

The fear of God can inspire us to forgive others. However, forgiveness is possible only through divine intervention. When we allow the Holy Spirit to guide us, our feelings of anger and resentment can be transformed into compassion. We begin to understand that those who hurt us may be spiritually malnourished and struggling with their mistakes. Forgiveness sets us free.

REMEMBERING OUR PAST SINS

One of the graces bestowed by the Holy Spirit is the ability to recall our past sins. Sometimes, buried and forgotten memories suddenly surface like a hidden iceberg. These memories may include images and past experiences that appear out of nowhere at any given moment. The Holy Spirit inspires these memories, which indicate that we must confess them and make amends.

We should write them down and address them as soon as possible.

THIRST FOR GOD

When seeking a connection with God, we might undergo a profound transformation. Suddenly, we are filled with an intense desire to attend Mass more frequently and unite ourselves with God in the Eucharist. We seek the word of God and long to confess our sins. We enjoy praying the rosary and yearn to discuss God with everyone around us. We become fascinated with movies about God and the Saints, and the world may label us as "fanatics." but we don't care.

We used to make fun of the old ladies who prayed after Mass. But now, we are part of this group of prayer warriors who come together before or after service. They are like the special squad of the Militant church, the "navy seals" helping save souls. They join the communal prayers of the clergy and the whole Church. Many times, we were in danger and were "saved by the bell." we used to consider ourselves "lucky" without knowing that we avoided such danger thanks to the intercessory prayers of these warriors.

As we thirst for God, our hearts are consumed by a desire to know and be closer to Him. When we lay in bed at night, our minds are filled with thoughts of His wonders and mysteries.

We wake up every morning with the same thirst for Him, eager to continue the journey of discovering who He is. As we walk with Him, we fall deeply in love with Him, just like when we fell in love with our first love. We become so consumed by Him that every thought and action is centered around Him. Similarly, we will desire our Lord with a much stronger force because our beloved will never disappoint us. To thirst for God is to desire Him; everything else in our lives takes a back seat.

STRIPPING AWAY OUR BAD HABITS

As we embark on our journey towards holiness, wonderful transformations take place in our lives. God purifies and heals our soul, filling it with His divine graces. Our hearts and minds become vessels of the Holy Spirit—a kind of possession, if you will.

This possession of the Holy Spirit is the complete opposite of diabolical possession. In the case of higher levels of demonic possession, the person is no longer in control of their actions. They become a slave to the evil spirit that has taken over their body and soul, causing them to behave in ways that are entirely out of character. They may become violent and aggressive and even display physical manifestations such as levitation or superhuman strength. However, the devil is a lousy imitator of God's divine power.

On the other hand, possession of the Holy Spirit is a beautiful and life-changing experience. As we are filled with the Holy Spirit, our lives are transformed in spectacular ways. We become more loving, compassionate, and forgiving toward others. We begin to see the world through a new lens. In short, we become the best version of ourselves through the possession of the Holy Spirit.

For Example:

Over time, if we consume alcohol frequently, we may gradually lose our enjoyment of it. Our bodies will start to reject drunkenness, and we may find ourselves drinking only on social occasions or even quitting drinking altogether. This same process can happen with other sinful habits as we begin to lose interest in them and eventually abstain from them completely.

If we used to enjoy music with violent or vulgar content, we may become weary of the melody and find it more like noise than music. We might even discover ourselves listening to classical, worship, or sacred music instead. Additionally, we will start paying more attention to the lyrics of the songs and the message of the movies.

The Holy Spirit will influence our choice of clothing, inspiring us to dress modestly. It is difficult to imagine a modern-day female Saint wearing tight-fitting clothes that reveal her breasts or a male Saint wearing earrings and sagging pants that expose his underwear unless he truly doesn't have access to more fitting clothes.

As we progress in our path to Holiness, we will gradually eliminate slurs, curses, profanity, and rude language from our vocabulary.

During cases of extreme demonic possession, individuals may exhibit extraordinary abilities such as moving objects, levitation, or displaying abrasions on their skin. In advanced states of holiness, one may experience bilocation, stigmata of Christ, mystical experiences, miracles, and healings. A holy person or Saint could become so Christ-like that their body becomes incorruptible at the moment of death. We see such miracles around the world with the preserved bodies of some Saints.

SATAN'S RETALIATION AND THE DARK NIGHT OF THE SOUL

> St. Teresa of Calcutta:
> "They tell me that God loves me, and yet the reality of darkness, coldness, and emptiness is so great that nothing touches my soul. Did I make a mistake by blindly surrendering to the Call of the Sacred Heart?"

The road to holiness is full of thorns. It is essential to remember that being in God's grace does not necessarily mean that we will be immune to life's adversities or that we will be given special privileges. The lives of the Saints, particularly the apostles, who were near the Lord, are a testament to this. Despite their unwavering faith and devotion, they were subjected to unimaginable suffering and brutal deaths, highlighting the fragility of human existence and the unpredictability of life.

- Matthew: killed by a sword wound.
- Horses dragged Mark through the streets until he died.
- Luke: He was hanged in Greece.
- John: He faced martyrdom when he was boiled in a huge jar of oil.
- Peter: He was crucified upside down on an X-shaped cross
- James: The leader of the Church in Jerusalem was thrown more than thirty meters from the pinnacle
- James, the son of Zebedee: he was beheaded in Jerusalem
- Matthias was stoned and then beheaded.

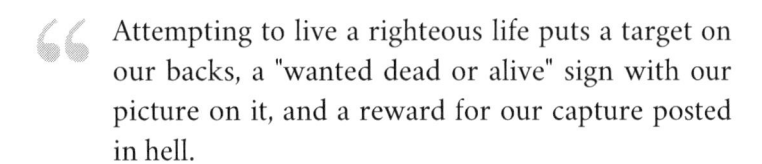

> Attempting to live a righteous life puts a target on our backs, a "wanted dead or alive" sign with our picture on it, and a reward for our capture posted in hell.

The battle has begun, and we must be prepared. We must remember that God allows these trials just as He did for His faithful servant Job.

> Saint Teresa of Avila to Jesus:
> "If this is how You treat your friends, it is no wonder You have so few!"

IMPORTANCE OF ACCEPTING SUFFERING

Suffering purifies the soul, and if accepted with obedience and humility, it can shorten the time spent in purgatory and help save souls. Those who are striving for holiness may face physical and spiritual attacks, not only against us but also against our loved ones and our pets. Therefore, it is important to include them in our daily rosary prayers for their safety and ours.

As we walk toward holiness, it is common sometimes to experience feelings of uncertainty and doubt. We may find ourselves questioning the effectiveness of our prayers, wondering whether they are being heard and answered. Sometimes, we may feel frustrated when everything seems to go wrong and progress feels backward. Concentrating on prayer can feel challenging, and we may struggle to feel a connection during communion or other forms of worship. It's not uncommon to have feelings of abandonment.

At times, we will likely experience periods of desolation, a spiritual battle with ourselves. These desolate times are essential to the purification process, where our love is refined. It is crucial to continue moving forward with trust in God during this phase despite the challenges. While these attacks may subside, it is important to remain vigilant and prepared, as they may resurface.

God will allow Satan to test us, just as wheat is sifted to separate the grain from the chaff. Therefore, no matter what happens, we should not let our prayer life or desire for holiness diminish.

Suffering is like rare and precious pearls that God throws at us from Heaven. These pearls may initially cause us pain and discomfort as they hit us, but if we take the time to examine them closely, we can find incredible value in them. Just as pearls are formed through the irritation and struggle of an oyster, our suffering can help us grow and persevere through difficult times.

We can use our suffering to fight against our enemy, Satan, by accepting it and offering it to God as reparation for our sins and humanity. We must grab those pearls and wear them around our necks just as a bride adorns herself for her beloved. All suffering has immense graces, even the smallest. We can save thousands of souls just by gladly accepting our suffering. For example:

When we accidentally cut our finger in the kitchen, instead of swearing or panicking, we take it as an opportunity to bless and thank God for allowing it to happen. We offer our pain as reparation for our sins. When we fall and hit ourselves, we do the same: bless, thank, and repair. These trials won't last forever, but they will come from time to time to test us. Let's Be Ready

OTHER SIGNS OF HOLINESS

Certain signs of holiness exist. For example, some people have the ability to "smell" sin. They can detect the unpleasant smell of mortal sins. On the other hand, others can smell the Heavenly presence, which is often described as the scent of roses.

Some individuals experience private revelations of the Virgin and Jesus. Additionally, some people can see the Eucharist in its spiritual form, with angels and the blood in the host. Some people have the gift of healing, while others can see spirits from purgatory. Furthermore, some experience the stigmata of Christ, which refers to the wounds of Christ in the hands and feet. Some holy people have also been said to have bodies that become incorrupt after death.

* * *

21

HOLINESS IN OTHER RELIGIONS

As human beings, we are all called to be holy, which means living a life of moral excellence, purity, and devotion to God. However, Holiness is a grace, and we cannot achieve it on our own. God completes our journey towards holiness at the end of our lives, as is God, who perfects our efforts according to the state of our souls.

Although people of different religious backgrounds can attain a certain level of holiness, they are at a disadvantage because they lack access to the sacraments. By living in mortal sin, they are spiritually malnourished, and in this natural state, the soul cannot enter Heaven, which is the ultimate goal of every Christian. Like most of us, they will have to pass through purgatory if they are saved by the grace of God and the intercession of His Church.

Many Christians from other religions are united with the body of Christ through baptism, assuming they used the Trinitarian formula:

"I baptize you in the name of the Father, and of the Son, and of the Holy Spirit."

baptism is the sacrament of initiation into the Christian

faith. These Christians are often baptized as adults, meaning they start their Christian lives with a squeaky-clean soul in adulthood. This state of their soul gives them a head start in their Christian journey towards holiness.

It's important to clarify that being Catholic and having access to the fullness of the truth doesn't necessarily make us more holy than anyone else. Absolutely not. Unfortunately, many Catholics don't take advantage of these resources, which can lead to spiritual malnutrition.

We are not the last glass of water in the desert nor the saviors of the world; we are merely servants of the servants of the Lord, instruments of salvation through the Eucharist.

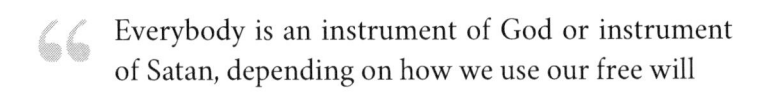

> Everybody is an instrument of God or instrument of Satan, depending on how we use our free will

However, since the Catholic Church was established by Christ, we are subject to its laws and teachings. As a result, we are instruments of salvation through His Church.

Whether Catholic or not, the possibility of going to Hell is equal for everyone; however, it's important to note that salvation is available to all, not just Catholics.

SALVATION IS FOR EVERYBODY

The Catholic Church infallibly teaches: "***Extra ecclesiam nulla salus***[1]," which means:

> "Outside the Church there is no Salvation"

The Congregation for the Doctrine of the Faith has deemed this statement infallible, meaning it is considered free from the possibility of being wrong. However, many people have misunderstood this dogma, believing that the Catholic Church claims that salvation is only available to Catholics. In reality, this statement means salvation is possible for everyone and that the Church is a means to attain that salvation.

It is considered a heresy called Feeneyism to declare that only Catholics can be saved. This belief originated from an American Jesuit priest named Leonard Feeney, who preached during the 1940s and 1950s that one must be a member of the Catholic Church to attain salvation. Feeney also claimed that individuals belonging to other religions, like Muslims, Jews, Hindus, atheists, and others, would be condemned to Hell for not being Catholics. As a consequence of his views, Feeney was excommunicated by the Church.

Let's read the Catechism of the Catholic Church 846:

> "846 How are we to understand this affirmation, often repeated by the Church Fathers? Re-formulated positively, it means that all salvation comes from Christ the Head through the Church which is his Body:
>
> Basing itself on Scripture and Tradition, the Council teaches that the Church, a pilgrim now on earth, is necessary for salvation: the one Christ is the mediator and the way of salvation; he is present to us in his body which is the Church. He himself explicitly asserted the necessity of faith and Baptism, and thereby affirmed at the same time the necessity of the Church which men enter through Baptism as through a door. Hence **they could not be saved who, knowing that the Catholic Church was founded as necessary by God through Christ, would refuse either to enter it or to remain in it.**"[2]

Here, the Church makes it clear that there is no salvation

outside the Church. However, the same paragraph clarifies that those who are not saved are those **who know and do not accept.** Even more interesting is paragraphs 847-848:

> "**847** This affirmation is not aimed at those who, **through no fault of their own**, do not know Christ and his Church:
> Those who, through no fault of their own, do not know the Gospel of Christ or his Church, **but who nevertheless seek God with a sincere heart**, and, moved by grace, try in their actions to do his will **as they know it through the dictates of their conscience** - those too **may achieve eternal salvation.**[3]

> **848** "Although in ways known to himself **God can lead those who, through no fault of their own, are ignorant of the Gospel**, to that faith without which it is impossible to please him, the Church still has the obligation and also the sacred right to evangelize all men."[4]

The statement suggests that individuals who are genuinely unaware of the truth but possess an earnest desire to comprehend and follow God's teachings will not be held accountable for their lack of knowledge. Despite their ignorance, they still have the potential to attain salvation.

DOES the Catholic Church contradict itself by affirming that salvation is only in the Catholic Church, yet also acknowledging exceptions?

. . .

THE CHURCH DOES NOT CONTRADICT itself, although it may seem that way to some. Let's look at a couple of documents:

Pope Leo II, in his encyclical Ubi Primum #14, May 5, 1824, speaks very clearly about salvation in the Church:

> " **It is impossible** for the most true God, who is Truth Itself, the best, the wisest Provider, and the Rewarder of good men, **to approve all sects who profess false teachings which are often inconsistent with one another and contradictory, and to confer eternal rewards on their members**. For we have a surer word of the prophet, and in writing to you We speak wisdom among the perfect; not the wisdom of this world but the wisdom of God in a mystery. By it we are taught, and by divine faith we hold one Lord, one faith, one baptism, and that no other name under heaven is given to men except the name of Jesus Christ of Nazareth in which we must be saved. This is why we profess that **there is no salvation outside the Church.**"[5]

This text highlights that the false teachings and beliefs of this world are not approved by God and do not lead to the truth. Members of these sects will not be saved through their heresies or false doctrines. The Church of Christ has the fullness of the truth and the only means of achieving salvation. In other words, the infidels will not be saved BY PRACTICING THEIR ERRONEOUS DOCTRINES; let's find out how they will be saved:

LET'S read what Pope John Paul II says in "The Seeds of the Word in the Religions of the World", September 9, 1998 #3

. . .

> 3. The Holy Spirit **It is not only present in the <u>Other religions</u> through authentic expressions of prayer**. Indeed, as I wrote in the Encyclical Letter*Redemptoris missio*, "the presence and activity of the Spirit affect not only individuals, but also society, history, peoples, cultures and religions" (n. 28).
>
> Normally, "through the **practice** of what **is good** in their own religious traditions, and **following the dictates of their conscience**, members of other religions respond positively to God's invitation and **receive salvation in Jesus Christ, even if they do not recognize Him as their Savior**"[6]

LET'S ANALYZE:

Here, the Holy Father explains that the Holy Spirit is present when prayers come from the heart.

> "The Holy Spirit **is not only present in other religions through <u>authentic</u> expressions of prayer**"

The Holy Spirit is present in all religions and cultures, not just in the Christian cultures:

> "The presence and activity of the Spirit affect not only individuals but also society, history, peoples, cultures and religions"

Suppose individuals from different religious backgrounds embrace the positive and virtuous aspects of their respective traditions and cultures, meaning taking the best of their knowledge and using their conscience to distinguish between right and wrong. In that case, they will respond positively to God's invitation:

> "Normally, "through the **practice** of what **is good** in their own religious traditions, and **following the dictates of their conscience**, members of other religions respond positively to God's invitation."

Even if they do not have sincere knowledge of God, these individuals can still attain salvation:

> "And **they receive salvation in Jesus Christ, even though they do not acknowledge Him as their Savior.**"

Oops, what happened here? Is The Church contradicting herself? Hmm, no, before you stone us, let us explain:

SALVATION IS attainable through the Catholic Church, either directly or indirectly. How does the world know who God is? Through His Church.

Who gathered the scriptures, compiled the books of the Bible, and gave it to the world? The Church, in the Year 382.

The same bible that religious sects have twisted and mutilated to fit their own agendas. These same sects claim to distrust the Catholic Church yet still rely on the same sacred scriptures that were compiled by the Church they so much hate. What is interesting to note is that none of the leaders of these sects were present during the compilation of the Bible; why? Because they didn't exist then, they only came into the picture more than a thousand years later with the birth of Protestantism in the 16th century, Year 1,517, to be exact.

Before the 1500s, everyone was Catholic. For 1500 years, we held the same doctrines and beliefs. But if Catholics were wrong, it begs the question: Did the apostles make poor decisions in selecting their successors? Where was the Holy Spirit during this time? Did Jesus institute a failure? I think not.

The world knows about God through His Church. Although contaminated by false doctrines in other sects, this knowledge is enough to draw man closer to God.

For instance, imagine an atheist who suddenly learns about God through a Protestant and decides to convert to Christianity. This person may not be aware of the Catholic Church or other churches with varying doctrines. Nevertheless, he is now a Protestant Christian and can achieve salvation —that is, **salvation from Hell**. Protestants have learned about God, the Bible, Baptism, marriage, and the Trinity through... THE CATHOLIC CHURCH. So yes, it's true. OUTSIDE THE CATHOLIC CHURCH, THERE IS NO SALVATION. Case closed!

CATECHISM OF ST PIUS X

> 29 Q. But if a man through no fault of his own is outside the Church, can he be saved?
>
> A. If he is outside the Church through no fault of his, that is, if he is in good faith, and if he has received Baptism, or at least has the implicit desire of Baptism; and if, moreover, he sincerely seeks the truth and does God's will as best he can such a man is indeed separated from the body of the Church, but is united to the soul of the Church and consequently is on the way of salvation"[7]

Let's take another example:

An atheist who was previously ignorant about religion and God. One day, he becomes friends with a devout Muslim who takes his faith seriously and practices it diligently by praying and fasting and does not practice violence. The atheist becomes curious about Islam and starts to learn more about it. Eventually, he became a Muslim and converted to the faith, going from being a Godless non-believer to a believer who can now attain salvation.

We wonder how Muslims learned about the Abrahamic God. How do they know that God must be worshipped, how did they learn the poses of prayer, and where did the knowledge of angels, Mary, and Jesus come from? They might say that their knowledge came from the Quran since Mohammed taught it, but how did Muhammad learn about God, Jesus, and the scriptures? He learned from the Jews and Christians. During the time of Muhammad, several stories and tales from Christianity and Judaism were circulating in the region. Who spread this knowledge to the world 600 years before the Quran even existed? It was the early Christians of the Catholic Church. Once again, *OUTSIDE THE CATHOLIC CHURCH THERE IS NO SALVATION.*

CLARIFYING SALVATION

Let us clarify the term salvation and analyze some scriptures. Salvation is for everyone: Titus 2:11

> *11 For the grace of God has appeared, bringing salvation to all,*[a]

. . .

NOTE that It does NOT say: "bringing salvation to all Catholic or Christian men."

> Luke 3:6
> *"And all flesh **shall see** the salvation of God.*

Here, it does NOT say: "all Catholic or Christian flesh."

> *Isaiah 52:10:*
> *The Lord has bared His holy arm*
> *before the eyes of **all nations**,*
> *and all the ends of the earth **shall see***
> ***the salvation** of our God.*

ISAIAH DOES NOT SAY: "and all Catholic or Christian nations shall see the salvation…"

SALVATION FROM WHAT? WHAT ARE WE SAVED FROM?

When someone says, "I am saved" or "he was saved," it is often understood as meaning "going to Heaven." This is the case of Protestants who think that the expression "to be saved" means going straight to Heaven. Let's clarify:

Salvation means *SALVATION FROM HELL*. That's it. Let us remember that purgatory is real. In this place, everyone is saved and holy because they can no longer sin and are in union with God. These souls will eventually join God in his kingdom.

When the Church says that a Protestant or non-Christian has the opportunity to be saved, this means that they have the chance to be saved from HELL, not necessarily going straight to Heaven.

> SALVATION FROM HELL is **FOR EVERYONE.**

MANY WILL WONDER about extremist Muslims, for example, who resort to violent actions and even suicide in the name of their religion. While this is a reality, it's important to recognize that there are also Muslims who are peaceful and do not do evil; they practice their religion, fulfill their religious obligation, and actively oppose and condemn the actions of violent Muslims.

Jews do not accept Jesus as the son of God. In their hearts, they believe that they are protecting the integrity of God and serving Him. For these individuals, Jesus is considered a heretic who founded a sect, and the Catholic belief in Jesus as God is seen as erroneous. It is difficult to imagine the outrage such a belief could instill in those who hold it so firmly. Despite their lack of knowledge, they could find salvation.

Protestants hold a belief system that rejects Our Lady and anything related to Catholicism. However, despite their rejection of these beliefs, many strongly believe that they are right in their stance.

These groups will not find salvation by practicing their religions; what will save them is a righteous and loving heart. Let us not forget that every human being has God's commandments written in their hearts.

> *Hebrews 10:16:*
> *16 And this is the testament which I will make unto them after those days, saith the Lord. **I will give my laws in their hearts, and on their minds will I write them:**"*

To those infidels with good intentions and thirst for God, God will give them mercy.

FOR INSTANCE, a Colombian priest once shared an anecdote about being stranded in a desert in the Middle East with a group of faithful individuals. They needed assistance, but there was no one around to help them. They began to pray, and to their surprise, a Muslim appeared on his camel to offer help. The Muslim explained that during his prayer, Allah had spoken to him and instructed him to go and help his "children" who were stranded in the desert.

Although "Allah" is not the Abrahamic God, this faithful Muslim believes that he is. Despite this, God was able to use him as an instrument to help this group in their time of need.

Let's consider the case of the unknown tribes that are still untouched by modern society and have no knowledge of the world beyond their immediate environment. They live in isolated communities where they have never been exposed to the teachings of any religion, let alone Christianity. It's possible that they still worship the sun or the moon, as they consider these celestial bodies as their deities and have no idea about the existence of the one true God. But the question arises: will they be condemned for their ignorance? Although these tribes have an ignorant heart, they desire to worship their Creator. because of their lack of knowledge, they worship what they believe to be God, such as the Sun. However, even though they are ignorant, they have God's commandments written in their hearts, and they know that stealing a neighbor's lamb is wrong and that killing a friend to take away his wife is wrong. God will judge them based on the love they gave and not on their lack of knowledge. However, since they are not nourished with the sacraments, there is a big possibility that they will also have to go through purgatory. All those infidels who are sincerely ignorant will be judged based on the love they gave.

Is purgatory also for Protestants and pagans?

VERY MUCH SO. Purgatory isn't just for Catholics. This is even in the scriptures. Read 1 Peter 3:19-20:

> *[19] In which also coming he preached to those **spirits that were in prison:***
> *[20] Which had been some time incredulous, when they waited for the patience of God in the days of Noe, when the ark was a building: wherein a few, that is, **eight souls, were saved by water.***"

According to the scriptures, Jesus preached to the pagans who were in purgatory, *"sojourned in the realm of the dead prior to his resurrection"* (Catechism 632)[8].

We know that the damned in hell cannot be preached to because they are already lost forever. Furthermore, we know that the only righteous ones during Noah's time were Noah and his family, who numbered eight individuals. All the others who perished in the flood were pagans. Since all souls in purgatory can no longer sin and are considered holy, it means that pagans, as well as people of other faiths, can attain salvation from hell and eventually ascend to Heaven.

BLESSED ANNE CATHERINE EMMERICH had a vision concerning Protestants in Purgatory:

> "I have seen Protestants in purgatory who lived piously in their religious ignorance. They feel abandoned, because no one prays for them."

> "It is true that among them there are many good ones, of whom I pity, but I see that they bear the stamp of their origin; they are separated from the Church and divided from each other. When devotion springs up in them, there arises at the same time in their souls a feeling of arrogance and deviation from their mother Church. They want to be pious, but they don't want to be Catholic. For this reason, even among the best, I see something defective, I see self-judgment, hardness, and pride."

THE CONSEQUENCES of Protestantism are devastating for souls because they lost the sacraments. Many are forgotten without prayers after their death.

* * *

22

SALVATION IN OTHER RELIGIONS

SALVATION FOR CATHOLICS

Being a Catholic does not automatically ensure salvation. For a Catholic to be saved, they must be a truly committed Catholic rather than merely identifying as one by tradition or title. If a Catholic abandons the faith and joins another religion, knowing that the Catholic Church belongs to Christ, they will not be saved. Leaving the faith because the church doesn't conform to one's lifestyle is deserting the militant church.

The document Lumen Gentium 14 refers to Catholics and how Catholics can be saved:

> "14. This Sacred Council wishes to turn its attention firstly to the Catholic faithful. Basing itself upon Sacred Scripture and Tradition, it teaches that **the Church,** now sojourning on earth as an exile, **is necessary for salvation.** Christ, present to us in His Body, the Church, is the one Mediator

and the unique way of salvation. In explicit terms He Himself affirmed the necessity of faith and baptism(124) and thereby affirmed also the necessity of the Church, for through baptism as through a door men enter the Church. Whosoever, therefore, **knowing that the Catholic Church was made necessary by Christ, would refuse to enter or to remain in it, could not be saved.**

They are **fully incorporated** in the society of the Church who, possessing the Spirit of Christ accept her entire system and all the means of salvation given to her, and are united with her as part of her visible bodily structure and through her with Christ, who rules her through the Supreme Pontiff and the bishops. The bonds which bind men to the Church in a visible way are profession of faith, the sacraments, and ecclesiastical government and communion. He is **not saved**, however, who, though part of the body of the Church, does not persevere in charity. He remains indeed in the bosom of the Church, but, as it were, only in a "bodily" manner and not "**in his heart**."(12*) All the Church's children should remember that their exalted status is to be attributed not to their own merits but to the special grace of Christ. **If they fail** moreover to respond to that grace in **thought, word and deed**, not only shall they **not be saved but they will be the more severely judged.(13*)**"[1]

The Catechism of the Church 837 tells us:

> "... Even though **incorporated into the Church**, one who does not however persevere in charity **is**

not saved. He remains indeed in the bosom of the Church, but 'in body' not 'in heart.'" [2]

Most of us will have to go through purgatory. We cannot be imperfect in the presence of God. However, we do have the necessary tools to go directly to Heaven. Sadly, many of us don't take advantage of it. Let's read what Our Lady says in her apparitions at Fatima:

> "You have to remember **that many souls are damned** because there is no one to pray and make sacrifices for them."[3]

> "There are **so many souls** that the justice of God condemns for sins committed against Me, that I come to ask for reparation; Sacrifice yourself for this intention and pray."[4]

St. Faustina was a holy person who received mystical revelations from Jesus. However, one day, Jesus appeared to her and saw the state of her soul. He told her that she owed him "a day in purgatory." This raises the question: what does this say about us? Many of us do not lead the kind of life St. Faustina did.

> Saint Faustina said in verse 36:
> "I immediately saw. the whole state of my soul as God sees it. I saw clearly everything that is not pleasing to God. I didn't know that we must be held accountable to the Lord, even for the smallest faults. What a moment! Who can describe it? Standing before the thrice-holy, Jesus asked me, "Who **are you?**" I answered, "I am Your servant, Lord." **You owe a day of fire in Purgatory.** I

wanted to throw myself immediately into the flames of the fire of Purgatory, but Jesus stopped me and said, "Would **you rather suffer now for a day or for a short time on earth?**" I answered: Jesus, I want to suffer in Purgatory, and I want to suffer on earth the greatest torments, even if it is to the end of the world. Jesus said, "**One thing is enough. You will come down to earth and suffer a lot, but for a short time and you will fulfill My will and My wishes. A faithful servant of Mine will help you fulfill it.** "[5]

SALVATION FOR PROTESTANTS

Protestants are in imperfect communion with the Church. However, it should be noted that even though communion is not perfect, it is still communion.

> The Catechism of Catholic Church 838 tells us:
>
> 838 "The Church knows that **she is joined in many ways** to the baptized who are honored by the name of Christian, **but do not profess the Catholic faith in its entirety or have not preserved unity or communion under the successor of Peter.**"322 Those "who believe in Christ and have been properly baptized are put in a certain, **although imperfect, communion** with the Catholic Church."[6]

Lumen Gentium 15 refers to the salvation of non-Catholic Christians. Here, it says that Protestants can be saved through connection with the scriptures imperfectly, yes, but salvation is possible:

> "15. The Church recognizes that in many ways **she is linked** with those who, being baptized, are honored with the name of Christian, though they do not profess the faith in its entirety or do not preserve unity of communion with the successor of Peter. (14*) For there are many who **honor Sacred Scripture, taking it as a norm of belief and a pattern of life, and who show a sincere zeal**. They lovingly believe in God the Father Almighty and in Christ, the Son of God and Saviour. (15*) They are consecrated by baptism, in which they are united with Christ. They also recognize and accept other sacraments within their own Churches or ecclesiastical communities. Many of them rejoice in the episcopate, celebrate the Holy Eucharist and cultivate devotion toward the Virgin Mother of God.(16*) They also share with us in prayer and other spiritual benefits. Likewise **we can say that in some real way they are joined with us in the Holy Spirit,** for to them too He gives His gifts and graces whereby He is operative among them with His sanctifying power...[7]

Although other religions may contain some elements of truth, the Catholic Church possesses the fullness of the truth:

> UNITATIS Redintegratio 3:
> "The separated brethren practice not a few acts of worship of the Christian religion, which, in various ways, according to the different condition of each Church or community, **can undoubtedly produce the life of grace**, and it must be confessed that they are apt to leave **open access to the communion of salvation.**

Therefore, even if we believe that separate churches and communities have their defects, they are not devoid of meaning and value in the mystery of salvation, because the Spirit of Christ **has not refused to use them as means of salvation**, the virtue of which derives from the very fullness of grace and truth entrusted to the Church.

The separated brethren, however, either individually or in their communities and their Churches, do not enjoy that unity which Christ wished to give to those whom he regenerated and vivified in a new body and in a new life, and which is manifested in Sacred Scripture and the venerable Tradition of the Church. Only through the Catholic Church of Christ, which is the general help of salvation, can the **full fullness** of the means of salvation be attained."[8]

Let's consider the case of a Protestant who is deeply committed to God and live his teachings. He actively engages in community service, shares his knowledge and faith with others, and believes that worshipping Mary is not right but does not hold any hatred towards her.

On the other hand, there is a Catholic who is lukewarm about his faith, holds grudges against his parents and siblings, seeks guidance from tarot cards, attends Mass out of obligation, mistreats his wife and children, and never confesses his sins. Both of them passed away. Who would be more likely to attain salvation? And if, by God's mercy, the Catholic makes a perfect contrition and is saved, who among them would be more spiritually advanced? Who would be placed on the highest level of purgatory and on the lowest?

SALVATION FOR NON_CHRISTIANS

the document Lumen Gentium 16 speaks of the salvation of non-Christians. Their salvation is possible if they are honestly ignorant (God puts the commandments in their hearts). Let's read the document Vatican II Lumen Gentium #16:

> "16 But the plan of **salvation also extends to those who acknowledge the Creator**, among whom are in the first place the Muslims, who, professing to adhere to the faith of Abraham, worship with us a one, merciful God, who will judge men at the last day. Nor is God himself far removed from others who seek the unknown God in shadows and images, since all receive from him life, inspiration and all things (cf.*Acts*17:25-28), and the Savior wants all men to be saved (cf.*1 Tm*2:4) **For those who, blamelessly ignorant of the Gospel of Christ and his Church, nevertheless seek God with a sincere hear**t and strive, under the influence of grace, to accomplish by works his will, known through the judgment of conscience, **can obtain eternal salvation** [33]. "[9]

Lumen Gentium 8:

> "This Church, established and organized in this world as a society, subsists in the Catholic Church, governed by the Successor of Peter and by the Bishops in communion with him.13] **Outside its structure are many elements of holiness and truth** which, as goods proper to the Church of Christ, impel us towards Catholic unity."[10]

. . .

St. Thomas Aquinas explains it more clearly:

> **Summa Theologica - Part IIIa - Question 8 Answer (to the objections) 1**
> The infidels, even if they do not actually belong to the Church, **do belong potentially.** Such power rests on two motives: first and foremost, the power of Christ, which is sufficient to save the whole human race; second, free will.[11]"

HERE, it explains that any non-Christian or pagan *(infidels)*, even if they are not Catholics *(actually belonging to the Church)*, have the possibility of becoming part of the body of Christ *(potentially)*. This is possible through the power of Christ and his desire to save all souls, as well as through their own free will. Their desire to know Him, despite their ignorance, enables them to become part of the body of Christ.

For instance, in the case of Muslims, let us read the Catechism of the Church #841:

> 841 The Church's relationship with the Muslims. "The plan of salvation also includes those who acknowledge the Creator, in the first place amongst whom are the Muslims; these profess to hold the faith of Abraham, and together with us, they adore the one, merciful God, mankind's judge on the last day."[12]

People from other religions won't attain Heaven by practicing their own religion but by their desire to unite with God.

Jews will not go to Heaven because they practice Judaism. Muslims will not attain Heaven by practicing their religion, nor a protestant by being a good Protestant. They are still in the wrong religion; however, having a desire to know God and the free will to seek Him can open up the possibility of salvation. If one sincerely believes they are following the truth and, in their ignorance, lead a just and righteous life within their means, they can attain salvation.

Muslims identify themselves with Abraham's faith. They profess and believe what they have been taught. Even though they worship God the Father, due to their ignorance and thirst for the Abrahamic God, they do not fully understand Him. Nevertheless, they can attain salvation through ignorance if they sincerely seek the truth. Catechism of the Church 843 tells us:

> 843 The Catholic Church recognizes in other religions that search, **among shadows and images**, for the God who is unknown yet near since he gives life and breath and all things and wants all men to be saved. Thus, the Church considers all goodness and truth found in these religions as "a preparation for the Gospel and given by him who enlightens all men that they may at length have life."[13]

In this paragraph, the Church recognizes the natural desire to know God in all men who seek Him among "shadows and images," meaning they believe in their hearts that they worship the correct God. The Church appreciates their good intentions despite their ignorance, and all the positive traits of these religions, including Hindus, Buddhists, etc., come from God.

But Hindus and Buddhists don't even believe in God. How can they attain salvation?

We have already given examples of how the Catholic Church

has the tools for salvation and imparts them either directly (Catholics) or indirectly by association with non-Catholics and pagans. For instance, Hindus venerate multiple gods and goddesses, but Brahma is recognized as their primary god, responsible for creating the universe. Their intention is to worship their creator, but their god is not the real God. These individuals, who are not Christians, do not have access to the sacrament of baptism. However, they can be baptized. The Catholic Church recognizes the importance of baptism and acknowledges three different types of baptism.:

- Sacramental Baptism
- Baptism of Desire
- Baptism of Blood

Catechism 1258:

> " 1258 The Church has always held the firm conviction that those who suffer death for the sake of the faith without having received Baptism **are baptized** by their death for and with Christ. **This Baptism of blood, like the desire for Baptism**, brings about the fruits of Baptism without being a sacrament."[14]

Baptism of blood refers to a scenario where a person dies for Christ before getting baptized. This was common in early Christianity when many believers were imprisoned in places where there was no water for baptism and then were executed by being thrown to the lions.

In the year 256, Cyprian of Carthage reported catechumens who were martyred before baptism:

> "They certainly are not deprived of the sacrament of baptism who are baptized with the most glorious and greatest baptism of blood, concerning which the Lord also said that he had 'another baptism to be baptized with' (Luke 12:50)" (Letters 72 [73]:22).[15]

The same thing happens with those who die with the desire to be baptized or to seek God and, for some reason, do not have time to be baptized and are on the verge of Death; these people will be automatically baptized by desire. Saint Thomas Aquinas writes about it:

> "...when a man wishes to be baptized but by some ill chance he is forestalled by death before receiving baptism. And such a man can obtain salvation without being actually baptized, on account of his desire for baptism, which desire is the outcome of faith that works by charity, whereby God, whose power is not tied to the visible sacraments, sanctifies man inwardly. Hence Ambrose says of Valentinian, who died while yet a catechumen, 'I lost him whom I was to regenerate, but he did not lose the grace he prayed for'" (*Summa Theologia* III:68:2, cf. III:66:11–12).[16]

If a Hindu person only knew Hinduism and lived a righteous life with the good intentions of his heart, he would be saved from going to hell. However, statistically speaking, he might have to go through purgatory to learn what he did not learn during his life on Earth.

. . .

Pope Pius XII, Encyclical Mystici corporis (1943)

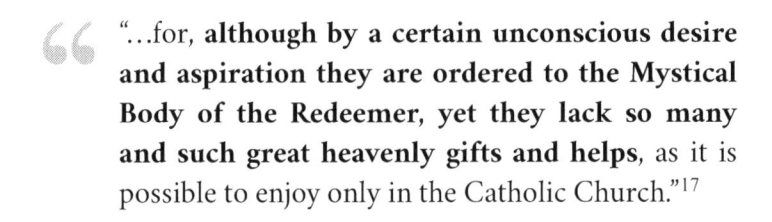

> "...for, **although by a certain unconscious desire and aspiration they are ordered to the Mystical Body of the Redeemer, yet they lack so many and such great heavenly gifts and helps**, as it is possible to enjoy only in the Catholic Church."[17]

PERFECT CONTRITION AND THE SACRAMENT OF CONFESSION

And what about confession? Both Protestants and pagans have no access to this sacrament and live their lives with mortal sins.

In cases of sincere repentance and desire to unite with God, man can attain perfect contrition even if he is not a Christian. The Catechism of the Church 1451-1452 explains to us what a perfect contrition is:

> "1452 When it arises from a love by which God is loved above all else, contrition is called "perfect" (contrition of charity). Such contrition remits venial sins; it also obtains forgiveness of mortal sins if it includes the firm resolution to have recourse to sacramental confession as soon as possible."[18]

> 1451 "Among the acts of the penitent, contrition appears in the first place. It is "a sorrow of the soul and a detestation of sin committed with the resolution not to sin again" [19]

Let's consider the scenario of passengers on a plane on the verge of crashing. Among the passengers is a pagan man who has led a life of sin, filled with adultery and drunkenness;

however, in the face of death, he experiences deep regret for the way he wasted his life and his lack of love for God. During these last few minutes of his life, he can achieve perfect contrition, which could save him from eternal damnation. This is possible because he was baptized with the baptism of desire and confessed his sins with perfect contrition.

* * *

23

KEEPING UP WITH OUR JOURNEY TO HOLINESS

DAY OR NIGHT

Now that we have adopted this new lifestyle, how can we sustain it? It is crucial to avoid situations that may lead to temptation. As someone once said, "demons come out at nightfall," indicating that most of our troubles occur after sunset. Nighttime is when parties and nightclubs open, and temptation is lurking everywhere; if we are not careful, we may lose control of our reasoning amid the noise and alcohol.

Most animals are inactive at night. Something about darkness causes creatures to hide away instinctively. What do they know that we do not? Upon reflection, we wonder if Jesus was nocturnal. Did he preach at night? If so, how late?

> *Mark 1:35*
> *"³⁵ And rising very early, going out, he went into a desert place: and there he prayed."*

Psalm 5:3:
"O Lord, in the morning you hear my voice;
in the morning I plead my case to you, and watch.it."

JESUS ALSO PRAYED AT NIGHT, but only during important events, such as when he chose his apostles.

Luke 6:12:
"12 Now during those days he went out to the mountain
to pray; and he spent the night in prayer to God."

In the Garden of Gethsemane, Jesus prayed late at night. However, the apostles fell asleep and could not pray with him, indicating they were not accustomed to staying up so late.

Finishing our day with our family at home is advisable, as it allows us to avoid situations that may lead to sin. Instead of going to a bar, attending adoration or watching a movie with our family would be more beneficial.

> The best way to avoid problems is to avoid situations where they are likely to occur

Although it may seem rigid or exaggerated, adapting our needs and schedules is worth considering.

CATHOLIC INNER CIRCLE

It is a good idea to consider joining Catholic groups, participating in their events, and offering our assistance. Having a social life with people who share the same spiritual goals and enjoy the same activities is more beneficial than surrounding ourselves with friends who engage in drug use or pagan practices. It is worth noting that although we can still have friendships with people of different faiths and backgrounds, it is always helpful to have spiritual support from people who share our beliefs and values.

When learning about our faith, it is crucial to ensure that we rely on trustworthy sources. We must refrain from seeking information on our history or doctrine from other Christian denominations. What can we learn from a denomination that has an incomplete Bible and a handicapped doctrine when we have the fullness of the truth in our Catholic church? It's like Americans learning about American culture from Chinese historians. Therefore, we should only refer to Catholic sources like videos, songs, movies, and documentaries for our learning unless we are researching or studying other denominations for teaching or correction purposes.

Being Catholic comes with a responsibility to use the tools the Church provides. It is important to catechize by setting a good example and always doing the right thing, planting seeds of faith in others.

* * *

24

REFLECTION

As Catholics, we are not guaranteed a place in Heaven. However, we have been provided with all the necessary resources to achieve it. Therefore, we will be judged more strictly because if we fail to use these resources correctly, we will have wasted them and the opportunities to help save souls and contribute to God's plan for salvation. To whom much has been given, much will be expected:

> *Luke 12:48:*
> *"⁴⁸ But the one who did not know and did what deserved a beating will receive a light beating. From everyone to **whom much has been given, much will be required;** and from the one to whom much **has been entrusted, even more will be demanded."***

Salvation is believed to be attainable only through the Catholic Church. Everyone connects with the Church through the sacraments and their knowledge of God. For instance, the Orthodox Church has valid sacraments that connect them to the Catholic Church. Likewise, Protestants are connected to the

Church through baptism, marriage, and the Bible, which proclaims the truth that has been revealed to them,

The Catholic Church revealed every truth about God, and only through her will we find the true way to salvation.

Being Catholic is not only a title but a great responsibility because we are Eucharistic instruments of reparation and we have been given all the fullness of the truth. Our souls are equipped to be instruments of Salvation for the world. God did not bestow us with this privilege to save only the souls of our relatives, the souls of people who benefit us, or the souls of those who like us. Each Catholic has the potential to save thousands of souls and positively change the world.

Many of us spend our lives solely focusing on ourselves and our personal affairs, and that's how we die.

How will we face our judgment before the Almighty? Have we used the tools of salvation entrusted to us? How many souls outside our flesh and blood have we helped? How many enemies have we saved? Have we acted against hunger, poverty, and injustice? Have we interceded on behalf of our brothers and sisters? Have we rescued souls from purgatory? God has given us all the necessary tools, but have we used them? Are we prepared to face our Creator?

Holiness should begin now because tomorrow is not guaranteed. We plan for retirement, although we might die tonite, but we forget to plan for eternity, which is our main goal. We only have today. Each day is a precious gift and an opportunity to turn around and do our duty.

So, what are you waiting for?

* * *

TAKE ME HOME

Through my brokenness and flaws,
Your glory is tearing down my walls.
Like peering through a foggy glass,
A glimpse of Heaven comes to pass.
Though my sins cause you pain,
Your grace surrounds me like a gentle rain.
You walk the path to Calvary's hill,
Despite my insults, you love me still.
I push you away, but you draw near,
Picking me up, casting out my fear.
Whispering softly, "Come back home, my dear."
Oh my Jesus, In your arms, worries disappear.
Through my tears, I say, "Yes, my Lord,
Take me in, raise me above."
Your love and mercy, a constant light,
I'm forever grateful for your endless fight.
Take me home, take me home now...

JZ. Maille

ABOUT THE AUTHOR

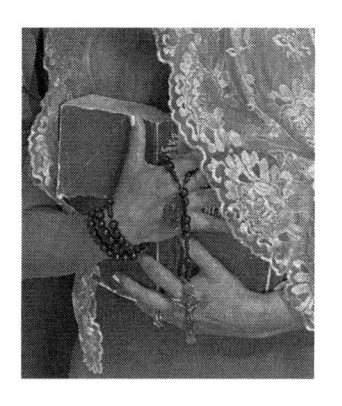

JZ Maille is a devout Catholic, passionate about Catholic history, theology, and apologetics. Her insatiable thirst for knowledge has equipped her with many skills, which she now harnesses to propagate the teachings of God and highlight the significance of leading a virtuous life. JZ is steadfast in her mission to shed light on the potential pitfalls of contemporary society, where unorthodox beliefs and practices often clash with Catholic doctrine, leading many to confusion. Driven by her profound understanding and fervor, JZ aspires to play a pivotal role in supporting Catholics on their arduous journey towards holiness, with the ultimate goal of helping them fully embrace and embody their faith.

Stay Holy…

facebook.com/thepathtoholiness
instagram.com/jzmaille

ALSO BY JZ MAILLE

Spanish Version of this book available:

EL CAMINO A LA SANTIDAD: Guía para católicos en un mundo pagano

AVAILABLE IN SPANISH
GET IT NOW!

NOTES

1. THE SAINTS OF THE CATHOLIC CHURCH

1. "Part Two Section Two The Seven Sacraments Of The Church Chapter One The Sacraments Of Christian Initiation Article 1 The Sacrament Of Baptism VII. The Grace Of Baptism." Vatican. Last modified April 20, 2024. https://www.vatican.va/content/catechism/en/part_two/section_two/chapter_one/article_1/vii_the_grace_of_baptism.html.
2. "Bible Gateway Passage: Leviticus 11:44 - Douay-Rheims 1899 American Edition." Bible Gateway. Last modified April 20, 2024. https://www.biblegateway.com/passage/?search=Leviticus+11%3A44&version=DRA. The *Douay Rheims 1899 American edition* will be used throughout this paper.

2. ATTAINING HOLINESS

1. "Bible Gateway Passage: John 3:5-6 - Revised Standard Version Catholic Edition." Bible Gateway. Last modified April 20, 2024. john. The *New Revised Standard Version* Catholic Edition Translation will be used throughout this paper.

3. THE GRACE OF GOD

1. "Catechism of the Catholic Church - Paragraph # 2023." Sc Borromeo. Last modified April 20, 2024. https://www.scborromeo.org/ccc/para/2023.htm.

4. THE ENEMIES OF HOLINESS

1. "SUMMA THEOLOGIAE: Lust (Secunda Secundae Partis, Q. 153)." NEW ADVENT. Last modified April 20, 2024. https://www.newadvent.org/summa/3153.htm#article4.

6. STEP ONE

1. "Open Wide Your Heart to the Extraordinary Graces of Divine Mercy Sunday." The Divine Mercy. Accessed April 20, 2024. https://www.thedivinemercy.org/articles/open-wide-your-heart-extraordinary-graces-divine-mercy-sunday.
2. EWTN. "Interview with Zachary King, 2022." *YouTube*. April 8, 2022. https://www.youtube.com/watch?v=Im8F63I0O9A&t=7s.

NOTES

3. "DIARY VI (1590-1803) - Divine Mercy in My SOUL." http://www.seraphim.my/divinemercy/diary/text/DiaryVI.htm

7. STEP TWO

1. "DIARY III (1001-1230) - Divine Mercy in My SOUL." Home of Seraphim. Last modified April 21, 2024. https://www.seraphim.my/divinemercy/diary/text/DiaryIII(1001-1050).htm.
2. Teresa of Avila. *The Way of Perfection*. Whitaker House, 2017.

8. STEP THREE

1. Santo, Lucia D. *Fatima in Lucia's own words: sister Lucia's memoirs*. Catholic Truth Society, 2017.
2. Santo, Lucia D. *Fatima in Lucia's own words: sister Lucia's memoirs*. Catholic Truth Society, 2017.
3. Santo, Lucia D. *Fatima in Lucia's own words: sister Lucia's memoirs*. Catholic Truth Society, 2017.

9. STEP FOUR

1. "Bible Gateway Passage: 1 Timothy 6 - Douay-Rheims 1899 American Edition." Bible Gateway. Last modified April 21, 2024. https://www.biblegateway.com/passage/?search=1+Timothy+6&version=DRA.
2. Liguori, Saint A., and Aeterna Press. *The True Spouse of Jesus Christ*. Aeterna Press, 2016.

10. STEP FIVE

1. "Catechism of the Catholic Church - IntraText." Vatican. Last modified April 21, 2024. https://www.vatican.va/archive/ENG0015/__P7O.HTM.
2. "Medjugorje - Our Lady's Messages From 1988 - English." The Medjugorje Web - Apparitions of the Virgin Mary in Medjugorje. Last modified April 22, 2024. https://www.medjugorje.org/msg88.htm.
   April 25, 1988

11. STEP SIX

1. St Louis De Montfort Church. Last modified April 22, 2024. https://sldm-fishers.org/documents/2021/11/Blessed%20Carlo%20Acutis%20e-book%20_final.pdf.
   page 23
2. https://centermirmedjugorje.com/the-five-stones/

NOTES

12. STEP SEVEN

1. "Why Pray in Latin? How Does Praying in Latin Benefit You?" Our Lady's Rosary Makers & Traditional Catholic Supplies Shop. Last modified May 15, 2017. https://www.virgosacrata.com/why-pray-in-latin.
2. "Sacrosanctum Concilium." Vatican. Last modified April 22, 2024. https://www.vatican.va/archive/hist_councils/ii_vatican_council/documents/vat-ii_const_19631204_sacrosanctum-concilium_en.html.
3. Santo, Lucia D. *Fatima in Lucia's own words: sister Lucia's memoirs*. Catholic Truth Society, 2017.
4. Santo, Lucia D. *Fatima in Lucia's own words: sister Lucia's memoirs*. Catholic Truth Society, 2017.
5. Santo, Lucia D. *Fatima in Lucia's own words: sister Lucia's memoirs*. Catholic Truth Society, 2017.
6. Santo, Lucia D. *Fatima in Lucia's own words: sister Lucia's memoirs*. Catholic Truth Society, 2017.
7. "Chapter IV: The Different Forms of Celebrating Mass." USCCB. Last modified April 21, 2024. https://www.usccb.org/prayer-and-worship/the-mass/general-instruction-of-the-roman-missal/girm-chapter-4.
8. https://www.vatican.va/archive/ENG0015/__P9K.HTM
9. https://www.vatican.va/archive/ENG0015/__P9K.HTM

13. STEP EIGHT

1. https://thericatholic.com/stories/st-cyprian,816?

16. STEP ELEVEN

1. "DIARY V (1322-1589) - Divine Mercy in My SOUL." Home of Seraphim. Last modified April 22, 2024. https://www.seraphim.my/divinemercy/diary/text/DiaryV(1501-1550).htm.
2. "DIARY IV (1231-1321) - Divine Mercy in My SOUL." Home of Seraphim. Last modified April 22, 2024. https://www.seraphim.my/divinemercy/diary/text/DiaryIV(1231-1321).htm.
3. "DIARY V (1322-1589) - Divine Mercy in My SOUL." Home of Seraphim. Last modified April 22, 2024. https://www.seraphim.my/divinemercy/diary/text/DiaryV(1551-1589).htm.
4. "DIARY IV (1231-1321) - Divine Mercy in My SOUL." Home of Seraphim. Last modified April 22, 2024. https://www.seraphim.my/divinemercy/diary/text/DiaryIV(1231-1321).htm.
5. "DIARY I (1-521) - Divine Mercy in My SOUL." Home of Seraphim. Last modified April 22, 2024. https://www.seraphim.my/divinemercy/diary/text/DiaryI(51-100).htm.
6. "DIARY II (522-1000) - Divine Mercy in My SOUL." Home of Seraphim.

NOTES

Last modified April 21, 2024. https://www.seraphim.my/divinemercy/diary/text/DiaryII(651-700).htm.

7. U.S. Catholic Church. *Catechism of the Catholic Church*, 2nd ed. Image, 2012.
8. *Code of Canon Law: Latin-English Edition*. Washington, DC: Canon Law Society of America, 1999.
9. STM House of Prayer. "St John Paul II on the Liturgy of the Hours." STM House of Prayer. Last modified October 22, 2019. https://www.liturgyofthehours.org/post/st-john-paul-ii-on-the-liturgy-of-the-hours.
10. "Divine Office – Liturgy of the Hours of the Roman Catholic Church (Breviary)." Divine Office – Liturgy of the Hours of the Roman Catholic Church (Breviary). Last modified April 22, 2024. https://divineoffice.org/general-instructions/.
11. LLC, CO N., Chicago, and IL (reg):. "~The Council of Trent - Session 25~." ~The Council of Trent~. Last modified April 22, 2024. https://www.thecounciloftrent.com/ch25.htm.
12. U.S. Catholic Church. *Catechism of the Catholic Church*, 2nd ed. Image, 2012.
13. "DIARY III (1001-1230) - Divine Mercy in My SOUL." Home of Seraphim. Last modified April 22, 2024. https://www.seraphim.my/divinemercy/diary/text/DiaryIII(1201-1230).htm.
14. Santo, Lucia D. *Fatima in Lucia's own words: sister Lucia's memoirs*. Catholic Truth Society, 2017.
15. U.S. Catholic Church. *Catechism of the Catholic Church*, 2nd ed. Image, 2012.

18. STEP THIRTEEN

1. "Code of Canon Law - Book IV - Function of the Church (Cann. 1244-1253)." Vatican. Last modified April 22, 2024. https://www.vatican.va/archive/cod-iuris-canonici/eng/documents/cic_lib4-cann1244-1253_en.html.
2. "Code of Canon Law - Book IV - Function of the Church (Cann. 1244-1253)." Vatican. Last modified April 22, 2024. https://www.vatican.va/archive/cod-iuris-canonici/eng/documents/cic_lib4-cann1244-1253_en.html.
3. "Medjugorje About Fasting." Medjugorje USA - Comprehensive Medjugorje Virgin Mary Website. Last modified April 22, 2024. https://www.medjugorjeusa.org/fastingmessage.htm.
    dec 25,1982
4. "Medjugorje About Fasting." Medjugorje USA - Comprehensive Medjugorje Virgin Mary Website. Last modified April 22, 2024. https://www.medjugorjeusa.org/fastingmessage.htm.
    July 21,1982

19. STEP FOURTEEN

1. "Compendium of the Catechism of the Catholic Church." Vatican. Last modified April 22, 2024. https://www.vatican.va/archive/compendium_ccc/documents/archive_2005_compendium-ccc_en.html.

21. HOLINESS IN OTHER RELIGIONS

1. "Extra Ecclesiam Nulla Salus." Wikipedia, the Free Encyclopedia. Last modified April 20, 2024. https://en.wikipedia.org/wiki/Extra_Ecclesiam_nulla_salus.
2. "Catechism of the Catholic Church - Paragraph # 846." Last modified April 23, 2024. https://www.scborromeo.org/ccc/para/846.htm.
3. "Catechism of the Catholic Church - Paragraph # 847." Last modified April 23, 2024. https://www.scborromeo.org/ccc/para/847.htm.
4. "Catechism of the Catholic Church - Paragraph # 848." Last modified April 23, 2024. https://www.scborromeo.org/ccc/para/848.htm.
5. XII, Pope L. "Ubi Primum." Papal Encyclicals. Last modified January 31, 2024. https://www.papalencyclicals.net/leo12/l12ubipr.htm.
   #14
6. "9 September 1998 | John Paul II." Vatican. Last modified September 9, 1998. https://www.vatican.va/content/john-paul-ii/en/audiences/1998/documents/hf_jp-ii_aud_09091998.html.
   #3
7. "Catechism of St. Pius X." EWTN Global Catholic Television Network. Last modified April 23, 2024. https://www.ewtn.com/catholicism/library/catechism-of-st-pius-x-1286.
8. "Catechism of the Catholic Church - Paragraph # 632." St, Charles Borromeo Catholic Church. Last modified April 23, 2024. https://www.scborromeo.org/ccc/para/632.htm.

22. SALVATION IN OTHER RELIGIONS

1. "Lumen Gentium." Vatican. Last modified April 23, 2024. https://www.vatican.va/archive/hist_councils/ii_vatican_council/documents/vat-ii_const_19641121_lumen-gentium_en.html.
2. "Catechism of the Catholic Church - Paragraph # 837." Last modified April 23, 2024. https://www.scborromeo.org/ccc/para/837.htm?ref=black catholicmessenger.org.
3. Santo, Lucia D. *Fatima in Lucia's own words: sister Lucia's memoirs*. Catholic Truth Society, 2017.
4. Santo, Lucia D. *Fatima in Lucia's own words: sister Lucia's memoirs*. Catholic Truth Society, 2017.
5. "DIARY I (1-521) - Divine Mercy in My SOUL." Home of Seraphim. Last

NOTES

modified April 23, 2024. https://www.seraphim.my/divinemercy/diary/text/DiaryI(1-50).htm.

6. "Catechism of the Catholic Church - Paragraph # 838." St. Charles Borromeo Catholic Church. Last modified April 23, 2024. https://www.scborromeo.org/ccc/para/838.htm.
7. "Lumen Gentium." Vatican. Last modified April 23, 2024. https://www.vatican.va/archive/hist_councils/ii_vatican_council/documents/vat-ii_const_19641121_lumen-gentium_en.html.
8. "Unitatis Redintegratio." Vatican. Last modified April 23, 2024. https://www.vatican.va/archive/hist_councils/ii_vatican_council/documents/vat-ii_decree_19641121_unitatis-redintegratio_en.html.
9. "Lumen Gentium." Vatican. Last modified April 23, 2024. https://www.vatican.va/archive/hist_councils/ii_vatican_council/documents/vat-ii_const_19641121_lumen-gentium_en.html.
10. "Lumen Gentium." Vatican. Last modified April 23, 2024. https://www.vatican.va/archive/hist_councils/ii_vatican_council/documents/vat-ii_const_19641121_lumen-gentium_en.html.
11. "SUMMA THEOLOGIAE: Home." NEW ADVENT. Last modified April 23, 2024. https://www.newadvent.org/summa/.
12. "Catechism of the Catholic Church - Paragraph # 841." St. Borromeo Catholic Church. Last modified April 23, 2024. https://www.scborromeo.org/ccc/para/841.htm.
13. "Catechism of the Catholic Church - Paragraph # 843." St. Charles Borromeo. Last modified April 23, 2024. https://www.scborromeo.org/ccc/para/843.htm.
14. "Catechism of the Catholic Church - Paragraph # 1258." St. Charles Borromeo. Last modified April 23, 2024. https://www.scborromeo.org/ccc/para/1258.htm.
15. Baptism of Desire | Catholic Answers Magazine. https://www.catholic.com/magazine/print-edition/baptism-of-desire
16. "SUMMA THEOLOGIAE: Those Who Receive Baptism (Tertia Pars, Q. 68)." NEW ADVENT. Last modified April 23, 2024. https://www.newadvent.org/summa/4068.htm.
17. "Mystici Corporis Christi (June 29, 1943) | PIUS XII." Vatican. Last modified June 29, 1943. https://www.vatican.va/content/pius-xii/en/encyclicals/documents/hf_p-xii_enc_29061943_mystici-corporis-christi.html.
18. "Catechism of the Catholic Church - Paragraph # 1452." St. Charles Borromeo Catholic Church. Last modified March 23, 2024. https://www.scborromeo.org/ccc/para/1452.htm.
19. "Catechism of the Catholic Church - Paragraph # 1451." St. Charles Borromeo. Last modified April 23, 2024. https://www.scborromeo.org/ccc/para/1451.htm.

THE PATH TO HOLINESS

Made in the USA
Columbia, SC
21 June 2024

8798c853-a813-4ed4-be0f-c9bc95d5cbf0R03